The Majorettes
ARE BACK IN TOWN!

## AND OTHER THINGS TO LOVE
## ABOUT THE SOUTH

Leslie Anne Tarabella

RIVER
ROAD
PRESS

New Orleans 2017

ISBN: 978-1-941879-16-0

The name and logo for "River Road Press" are trademarks of River Road Press LLC and are registered with the U.S. Patent and Trademark Office.

For information regarding permission to reproduce selections from this book, write to Permissions, River Road Press LLC, PO Box 125, Metairie, Louisiana 70004.

For information on other River Road Press titles, please visit www.riverroadpress.com.

Cover design by Robert M. Tarabella
Cover photograph by *The Decatur Daily*, www.decaturdaily.com

Printed in the United States of America

Published by River Road Press
PO Box 125
Metairie, LA 70004

For Robert,
my perfect Southern (at heart) gentleman.

# Contents

# Dearest Readers...

I started writing short stories on a blog several years ago, and the local newspaper contacted me to ask if I'd like to write a weekly column. From there, I moved on to write for AL.com and now my column appears in the Sunday editions of the Mobile *Press-Register, Birmingham News,* and *Huntsville Times* as well as in the *Mississippi Press.*

I enjoy writing about things I love, which is pretty much anything in the South, including good manners, church, food, and children (who surprise us by growing into spirited, funny teenagers). I especially love to think and write about what all Southerners love, and that is anything shiny or sparkly!

Southerners love glittery, sparkly things that match our shiny personalities. We love to celebrate life and look for reasons to throw a party. Southern ladies love tiaras and glittery sorority posters proclaiming, "Phi Mu rocks!" or "Tri Delta loves their pledges!" We love rhinestones, sequins, and twinkling stars in the night sky. Southern men love shiny football trophies to carry over their heads, flashing fishing lures, and gleaming truck wheels. They also appreciate lovely ladies with sparkling eyes and dazzling smiles.

I attended a birthday party for a ninety-eight-year-old friend who was born in Atlanta, played at her mother's feet while visiting their friend Margaret Mitchell, then moved and grew up in Mobile. For her birthday dinner, she wore a fabulous silvery, shimmery top that we all found captivating. There was even a hot discussion: "Is it gold or silver?" Whatever it was, she looked like a gorgeous Hollywood star. Ladies like this are experts at celebrating life with a little sparkle.

Southerners know how to take a modest morsel and turn it into a jubilant banquet. Every day we live in the South is reason enough for a party. That's why we have so many serving dishes and cabinets full of china and crystal. You never know when forty of your closest friends will show up with a cooler full of fish or slabs of meat to grill. We'd never be without two or three deviled egg plates, because we have been raised to know a plate of deviled eggs or a good homemade cake can turn any dull meeting into a rollicking party. We never go far without taking along food for fear of missing an opportunity to revel in the moment.

God has blessed us with balmy weather, camellias of every color, boiled peanuts, fields of cotton, and lilting accents. We feel honored that God chose us to bestow the gifts of delicious corn with the sparkly names of Silver King and Silver Queen. We also have the comfort of seersucker and the beauty of magnolias. No one else gets to hear such poetic language every single hour of the day. No one else gets to have NASCAR. No one else was given the good sense to put salty peanuts in their sweet Co-Colas. We are favored. We are loved. We have huge reason to sparkle, shine, and celebrate. A mere cheerleader won't do. We need glittery, shiny, happy, high-stepping majorettes!

Anytime we can have sequins, tiaras, rhinestones, and fire twirling, it makes a regular old day a joyful event. We are happiest when we are at a party. Southerners have a gift for making a soirée out of a simple trip to the shoe store. We can create a festive occasion in line at the post office. We can turn painting an elderly neighbor's house into the biggest shin-dig of the year. When we find our lost dog, we throw a party. When I had my pearls restrung, I got the girls together for lunch to show them the excellent craftsmanship. Did the Little League team win their championship game? Then we must have a parade, complete with antique fire engines, confetti, horses, the high school band, and . . . majorettes!

Swinging on the front porch with friends somehow leads to singing, telling jokes, and running to get the neighbors so they can join in. We can go fishing and feel as elegant as if we were at a formal gala. We can attend a simple country church service and leave crying tears of joy as if we've just seen the Passion acted out on Broadway. Anything can lead to a joyful celebration.

Why, even Southern funerals are often full of celebration for a life well lived and for the good memories left behind. Southerners know how to do a funeral right. Rows of tables hold the homemade food, and ladies wear appropriate black dresses (not cocktail glittery black; this is the one time we know to suppress the sparkle). White pearls show up nicely against the black, symbolizing the light and hope amidst the darkness. Tables swaying under the weight of the food hold casseroles, cakes, pies, fried chicken, and okra, the Southern vegetable that starts a party in your mouth every time.

Every now and then, my darling Yankee husband is the subject of my stories and only serves to accentuate and remind me of the interesting characteristics of the different regions in America. I grew up in a military town where many of my friends came from other parts of the country, so regional differences have always fascinated me, and I like trying to figure out where someone is from based on their accent or word choices. Do they say, "lightning bug" or "firefly?" Do they "press" the button or do they "mash" it?

My husband has a great ear for accents and once, when we were in California, asked a woman if she was from North Alabama, and sure enough, she said, "Yes, I grew up in Huntsville. How did you know?" "You sound just like my mother-in-law from down the road in Hartselle," he replied. She laughed and looked at me and said, "Your mama is from Alabama? I knew I liked you!" Such a perfect Southern response, and, of course, we were instant friends.

I guess I'm thinking about our regional characteristics more these days because suddenly, it's cool to be Southern. Everyone wants to drink out of a Mason jar and get married in a barn. Once teased for our accents and laughed at for being like *Hee Haw,* now it's hip to be Southern. The internet features thousands of beautiful ideas for serving sweet tea, and everyone wants to say "y'all," even if they don't know how or when to say it. Newcomers to our area desperately try to fit in. While some have succeeded and have developed a hankering for collard greens and friendliness, others can't get the hang of it and still look the other way when passing on the street and have blown our passion for monograms way out of proportion—quite literally. They think that just because they have stuck a two-foot-tall vinyl monogram on the back window of their minivan, they've suddenly turned themselves into Scarlett O'Hara.

The funny thing to me is that many of the Southern traits I write about have been brought to my attention by Northerners or Midwesterners who have moved here and are amazed we put bows on everything, or they let me know that absolutely no one here knows the correct use of a car horn. Things I assumed were standard and normal they seem to find odd, proving to me that our newcomers love to sum us up as much as we take sport in evaluating them.

Differences can be good. I love knowing that Texas chili is different from Mississippi chili. For one thing, Texans hate beans in chili. Why is that? I also love knowing that when I'm in Massachusetts, I can get a lobster roll like nowhere else in the world. And I love how people in Boston say good things are "wicked." In the South, we only use "wicked" to describe the devil or the other team's coach (they are often one and the same). Differences make us interesting. They also narrow down and highlight our similarities, which in a way unites us.

Understanding that our new neighbors from Michigan find it irritating when we leave buckets of zucchini on their doorstep can lead us to a later conversation where we discover they actually love tomatoes and would like for us to help them start a garden. Not knowing anything about Southern humidity, soil, or insects, they'd be thankful for any tips we could offer. See? Now we're all friends with lots of tomatoes. It doesn't get better than that!

The liturgy of celebration defines who our families are and what it is we value. The process of rejoicing over the average day is yet another quality and method of survival that has been passed down through generations of optimistic Southerners.

If the South dwells within you, and you don't just dwell in the South, then you certainly have the positive penchant for a happy outlook somewhere deep inside your heart. But if you are new to our region, or if you have lost your spark for a joyful life, it's never too late to join us at the party. Rejoice in all that is good and thank God you live in such a charming, delightful place. Pour a big glass of iced tea, sit on the porch with nice people, and put a smile on your face, not just a sticky monogram on your car. Don't crinkle your nose while watching others have all the fun. Anyone can join in. A festive attitude and grateful heart isn't exclusive to Southerners; we only perfected it. And if all efforts fail, and you still think it's too hot here and we're all a bunch of barbarian rednecks, then celebrate the fact that moving trucks run in both directions! (Forgive me, Father.)

Some folks call themselves Southern just because of where they were born or where the moving van dropped them off. Others know they are Southern because the South lives within them. You can see the sparkle in their eyes when they see a friend walking their way or someone mentions a fish fry with hushpuppies and grits or suggests, "Let's go out and sit on the porch." The answer is never "I'm watching my cholesterol," or "It's too hot."

No matter where their families originated, my readers are the dearest, most loyal people who are all Southern at heart. You have given me kind feedback and encouragement to put your favorite stories into this book. I'm just tickled to death to share these columns with you and hope you enjoy them. We value our beautiful lives, we appreciate all things lovely, and we celebrate life—with dinner on the grounds, balloon festivals, tailgating at the stadium, mullet tosses, rodeos, car races, beauty queens, and lots of sparkly baton twirling. Thank you so much for spending time celebrating with me, and bless your heart for reading this book!

# I.
## Our Charming Southern Ways

When speaking of the South, people often use the word "charming." We honor equal opportunity rights when it comes to charm. There's no restriction on age, race, or gender. Every single one of us can mow you down with our charm and you'll beg us to do it again. Real Southerners know that in order to be charming, you must be genuine, real, and bonafide. If you try to fake charm, we'll spot you a mile away and know you aren't to be trusted (and you probably wear white shoes in December). With great charm comes great power and responsibility. Don't use it for evil. Charm should never harm.

# The Tempo of Our Tongues

A report from the office of Drawl & Y'all, LLC revealed the typical American speaks approximately 145-160 words per minute. New Yorkers tend to speak 160-180 words per minute, whereas in the Deep South, the average is around 135 words per minute.

"Maybe God made Southerners speak more slowly as a gift to the rest of the world so our lilting and melodic words can be savored and better appreciated by those who are fast talkers . . ." or at least that's what cousin Rosie Belle from Robertsdale told me. She fusses at me all the time because I'm a rare breed in these parts. I am a fast-talking Southerner.

To make things worse, I married another anomaly of nature, a slow-talking Northerner. It's yet another category where we have the golden opportunity to drive each other plumb crazy.

Perhaps the reason for my fast-speak is that I was the first girl born into an extended family heavily dominated by males (mainly politicians, pirates, and preachers) where conversation was always loud and lively. I learned that if I had anything to say, I needed to make it good, say it fast, and get out of the way.

Mama blames my rapid communication pattern on the influence of the Yankee volunteers in the church nursery who had moved South to staff the nearby Stennis Space Center and carry out their plan of maniacally destroying the developing speech patterns of baby belles and beaus in the area.

My poor in-laws, who grew up in New Jersey and NYC (bless their hearts), already have trouble interpreting my drawl, but the rapid-fire way I deliver the message makes it even worse. I try to slow it down, but when I'm excited, I take off and it's hard for them to decipher a thing.

"This ham's so salty, it makes me swell up like a tick on a hog," I say in two seconds flat. With their noses scrunched up and heads tilted to one side they ask, "Your mom's so faulty, she sells sticks on a cog?"

I found comfort when I learned I'm not the only Southerner with a Talladega tongue. My dearly beloved Florida State University football coach, Jimbo Fisher, is famous for driving the press crazy with how fast he speaks. Reporters and especially those who have the job of transcribing his interviews can't seem to keep up with his mouth. When the national press saw him put peanuts in his bottled Co-Cola, they flipped out. Jimbo tried to explain to the foreigners it was a typical Southern treat, but they didn't get a word of it and instead reported the coach had a nutritional deficiency.

Although people complain they can't understand me, I have to say I tend to agree with many from the Northeast (*gasp*) who say it's just as hard to understand someone with a slow molasses mouth. You tend to forget what they are talking about when it takes them twenty minutes to get to the point. The Southern accent is a thing of beauty I could listen to all day, but there are occasions when even I have wanted to pour a strong espresso down the throat of someone and scream, "Just say it! Say it already!"

Even though my sweet husband and I have had years to practice the art of mixed-marriage conversation—and believe me, it took some practice—there are times his slow responses still throw me for a loop.

"Jeet yet?" I'll yell from the kitchen.

". . . (*nothing*)," he says.

(*Louder.*) "I said, 'Didjaeat yet?'"

"I heard you the first time!"

"Then why didn't you answer me?"

"I was getting ready to answer, but I had to think about it first."

Who on the green earth has to stop and think about whether or not they've eaten anything?

Taking time to think about what we say before we speak? Why, that's a novel idea most opinionated Southerners (and Northerners) have never considered, no matter what the tempo of their tongues may be.

# Hope of the South

Until recently, I've always felt safe in the South. Instead of staying out of each other's business, we make it a point to know one another, which creates a feeling of security. We make eye contact, then smile and say hello when we pass on the streets. We carry chicken casseroles to sleepy parents with new babies, offer plastic Cool Whip bowls full of homemade soup to a friend who is down with the flu, and welcome new folks to town with the obligatory invitation to visit our church.

But for the first time ever, I've felt the chill of fear creep into my own Southern home. All of us have watched helplessly as terrorism has crossed the ocean to first grab New York City, then waft its stench into every neighborhood, rural farm, and mountaintop home in America. We're now infected coast to coast with worry that keeps us awake at night.

Lately, when I hear sirens, I don't automatically think a parade is coming through town. Like many of you, if I hear a commotion now, a knot forms in my stomach and I worry about the children at school or those shopping downtown.

I was surprised when I recently caught myself searching for the exits at the local movie theater then flinching when someone entered after the film had begun. In familiar restaurants, I've started scanning the faces of people I don't recognize and wondering who they are.

How can our homespun communities suddenly be infiltrated by fear? We're the friendly region of the country, where people linger and laugh with neighbors on front porches. We're the easygoing birthplace of soft drawls and sweet tea, not suspicion and distrust.

As Americans are adapting to this cautious new way of life, surely Southerners will be the last region to wave the flag of surrender and give in to anxiety and despair, not because of our stubborn pride, but because we have a secret weapon. And no, it isn't our love of guns or a good fight. This weapon has been rooted in us by generations of hardworking, faithful people; it is our deep abundance of hope.

Southerners are the greatest of all optimists, who hope for everything from producing a bumper crop to reeling in the big one. After being defeated in every single game of the season, we'll utter the most hopeful words known to man: "Just wait till next year."

Hope is different than a wish and far better than dumb luck. Southerners are born with hearts seeded with hope and nurtured with Dixie Cups full of watery grape Kool-Aid at Vacation Bible School. None of us are too far removed from the generation that taught us lessons of hope through their stories of meager beginnings that resulted in new homes with running water, thriving businesses, and sometimes the family's first college degree.

The art of taking something ugly and transforming it into a thing of beauty is even evident in our speech. Where some regions speak with abrupt, negative tones, Southerners can sugarcoat the worst kind of news, dip it in optimism, and spin it to the point of making you beg to hear it again.

If love and faith are the heart and soul of the South, then hope is the breath of our lives. Without hope in something greater, we may as well live in a place where no one holds doors for ladies or makes new friends while waiting in line at the post office. Our kindness and friendly mannerisms are based on hoping for a better world, hoping we'll find something exceptional right around the corner, or as a well-known Southern belle once put it, "After all, tomorrow is another day."

While the headlines tell us it's going to be a "year of fear," I'll remember my roots and cling to hope: hope for wise leadership, hope in a strong military, hope for the safety of our brave law enforcement officers, and absolute hope in my God, because that's the core of our fearless hope of the South.

# Are Southern Women Prettier?

You've heard it before but were afraid to say it yourself for fear of sounding boastful: Southern women are prettier than others. But wait just a cotton-pickin' minute. Is it true? Are we really prettier? I'll let you in on a little secret. We're not. Everyone just has that illusion because the truth is, we try harder. Our secret weapon for loveliness, passed down by generations of Southern ladies, is our ability to make the best out of what we have or, in other words, our "effort."

The twins Bayer and Bryant were mad at their mama for spending so much money on their little sister, Crimpsen. "Mama, you know me-n-Bryant need new baseball gloves, but you said we'd have to wait, and now she gets to sign up for dumb old Miss Carol's School of Baton Twirling? That ain't fair!"

"First of all, young man, don't say 'ain't.' Second of all, it's 'Bryant and I.' And third of all, girls need these classes so they'll know how to carry themselves in public someday. If she can learn to twirl, march, and smile at the same time, there's nothing that can stop her."

The children's mother was right. Even though Dixie darlings have the reputation for being the most beautiful women in the world, the truth is, we work at it, starting at an early age. Just like Granny produced a feast from a cup of flour and a skinny chicken during the Depression, if she works hard, Beulah Mae can clean up real nice-like and get a date for the dance.

The first line of the Southern classic *Gone with the Wind* comes right out and admits it: "Scarlett O'Hara was not beautiful, but men seldom realized it when caught by her charm as the Tarleton twins were." Those Tarleton twins, God love them. They fell for the oldest trick in the book. Scarlett had spent all morning squeezing her size two self into a size zero corset, pinched her cheeks, and worked on her curls with a hot iron from the fire. She was weighted down in layers and layers of her green-flowered frock, and after all that effort and using the best bait possible, she reeled in the prize catch: cute, red-headed twins. You go, girl.

Even with half the effort of Scarlett, the homeliest sister in the house, who can eat corn on the cob through a picket fence, can boost her appeal by taking time to primp and pamper, bless her heart. A little dab here, a little fluff there, wrestle her into some Spanx, and, honey, she's a looker.

"I've heard," whispered Nancy Jean, "there are some girls who smear on Chapstick and walk out of the house."

"Do tell!" gasped Johnetta Faye.

"Yes, and they also have something called a 'practical haircut.'"

If you've ever traveled with a Southern female, you've witnessed the enormous effort involved in getting "the look." Eight suitcases holding a variety of hair products, hair appliances, and hair accessories as well as individual cases of skin products and makeup doodads must be loaded into the car. The other cases are full of shoes.

I remember when I stopped on the trails at the Grand Canyon and reached in my bag for my cordless, butane-powered curling iron. As I perched on a rock and touched up my hair, others were obviously impressed because they stood there with their mouths hanging open like a bass fish.

Although we're a radiant bunch, don't think our beauty defines us. Once we understand the power of hard work and applying the needed "fluffing" to those areas that are lacking, it opens up a new world of appreciation for hard work and effort in other areas as well. Remember, Scarlett went on to work her hands to the point of callouses, but it paid off down the road with her own successful business and the finest home in all of Atlanta. "Effort" (along with hairspray and Lycra) is a Southern woman's secret weapon, indeed.

# To Be Sixteen in the Summer in the South

Summer in the South for a sixteen year old consists of parents who bother him more than the heat and days filled with friends, food, and future adventures waiting just around the corner.

He's too old to stay home with his mama but not yet old enough to be set totally free. It's a summer for finding a real job in the real world and discovering how very real part-time pay and full-time taxes are. A new driver's license in his wallet gives him the itch to explore beyond the regular boundaries of the city limit signs, but the new reality of having to pay for gas keeps him close to home. The guys proudly bring their cars over for a wash, wax, and polish session and when his mom brings out a pitcher of lemonade, he pretends to spray her with the hose. She says she's going to yank a knot in his tail and they all have a good laugh. The old truck will get dirty again in a few hours when the boys drive to the river to cool off and swing on the rope that was there when their dads were teenagers, probably about a hundred years ago.

Rolling out of bed before the humidity becomes unbearable, he cuts the grass then goes to his Sunday school teacher's house and joins other kids from his youth group to paint, rake, and wash, knowing the only pay will be a plate of homemade cookies. They're fine with this arrangement because just being with friends is the best part of the day, and once again the lesson of "doing unto others" grows even stronger.

For paying jobs, they stock shelves at the market, wash dishes at the downtown café, and work as the dreaded cage cleaner for the local vet. Having known them since they were babies, their bosses tell their parents what fine men they'll be someday, but the boys wonder why no one can see the men they already are.

After work, they meet for milkshakes and talk about how someday they'll have exciting jobs they love, making more money than they can spend. That's when one says he'll get out of this small town and live in a big city in a modern loft with glass tables, no dumb antiques to dust and no yard to mow. The others slurp their frosty treats and agree this is a great idea.

Little do they know, at that very moment, there's a sixteen year old in a faraway city discussing what it would be like to sit in a field untouched by glaring lights and gaze through the shadows of twisted oaks, illuminated by lightning bugs below and the twinkling stars above. He imagines a place where everyone speaks to one another and the most dangerous thing in town is a cottonmouth slithering through the vegetable garden.

The bright white moon shines on a red dirt road that somehow looks different at night, and the cows lift their heads when they hear the teens singing and laughing at the top of their lungs. Over the ruckus of crickets and frogs, there's time to discuss important things like the first presidential election they've been old enough to understand or the girl one of the boys just noticed who has a nice laugh and swears he once made her cry in preschool.

The boys who play football have to leave early to get a good night's sleep because even in the summer, there's early-morning practice since there's a good chance the state championship may be within reach this year.

The long days of summer stretch on forever with no concept of what life will soon become. College, careers, and marriage will soon arrive, and one day, a grown man will step out of his air-conditioned office and deeply inhale the late summer heat. It will be then, for a brief moment, that he's reminded of his teenage friends and what it was like to be sixteen in the summer in the South.

# We Speak the Truth

Jill just came right out and said it. Her Disney-esque eyes were wide with sincerity as she made a grand gesture of kindness. But her lovely offer was followed up with, "I'm not just being Southern. I really mean it." I blinked and took in the full value of what she had just said then doubled over laughing.

Since when did "speaking Southern" equate to empty, meaningless promises? Our kind words have always been sincere, and thoughtful offers were meant as the gospel truth. Handshakes sold businesses and a promise was something kept.

But now I wonder, does the rest of the world really doubt a Southerner's word and consider it to be nothing but fluff and emptiness? Just because we drop the endings from our words doesn't mean we drop the intent.

Our expressions may have an extra dose of "flowerdyness," but our word is good as gold. If we tell you your caramel cake is "as light as the angels," we mean it. If you overcooked the icing, we'll just say it's "mighty good (effort)." No offense, but truthfulness nonetheless.

"Bless her heart" used to mean just that: "Dear God in heaven above, please look down on this poor soul and bless her. Bless her to the core and bless her heart that beats its true love for you. Bless . . . her . . . cotton . . . pickin' . . . heart."

But now, someone in the world of "people we don't know who change the rules" has decided that "Bless her heart" means "She's a real witch." I suspect these are also the asinine people who decided everyone should wear white shoes in October and preteen girls' Halloween costumes should be sexy. That's just crazier than a pet coon.

When I ask for blessings on someone's heart, it's the real deal. If I want to say she's a witch, well, there's a way of saying that too—something along the lines of "She's meaner than a hot skillet full of rattlesnakes." This is followed by an all-sincere "Bless her heart" because people with a mean streak are in dire and immediate need of having their hearts truly blessed.

Those interacting with Southerners have to learn to read, or listen, between the lines. We mean what we say and say what we mean but throw in extra words—and syllables—to express ourselves and often soften the blow of bad news.

When I was a newlywed, I was startled and somewhat offended when my cranky Yankee husband would give me sharp answers like "yes" or "no." "Does this dress look okay?" was never answered with "Oh sweetie pie, that dress looks good enough on you to make a grown man cry. Mmm-hmm, mighty fine indeed!" Instead, I got a "sure." No extra words, just a cut-to-the-chase response. And because he was so abrupt and brief, I was insulted and didn't believe a word he said.

The notion that two groups of people don't believe each other because of how many or how few words they use in conversation may explain why our congressional delegates are often at odds. Perhaps they're all trying to say the same thing, but it just comes out differently depending on which part of the country they represent. Flowerdy vs. flippant. Beauty vs. brusque. Vibrant vs. vague. It's a language barrier we may never overcome. And that's a problem bigger than your Aunt Annie's fanny after a long car ride.

# The Majorettes Are Back in Town!

My prediction for the coming year is that America will experience a definite upswing in all categories. The overall population will be happier, businesses will prosper, and gravy will be lump free. I know this to be true because of the main indicator I've tracked for years: the Majorette Factor.

Several years ago, while attending a parade, I noticed there wasn't a single majorette. The marching band had flag corps members, but there was no majorette anywhere. "What is this world coming to?" I wanted to know. "America is losing sight of what's important. Twirling batons make the world a better place!" Sure enough, shortly after my observation, the USA plummeted into a huge recession, country music lost its focus, and the bee population almost vanished.

There was a time when all little girls either took dance or baton lessons. I chose to be a majorette because my hands were more coordinated than my feet and the baton could double as a weapon, which fascinated me. Every week, my mother would take me to the Myrtle Grove YMCA and Miss Rita would teach us how to twirl. We wore blue sparkly costumes our mamas sewed for us and marched in parades all over town.

Southern girls love to be majorettes because everything about them is so sparkly—much more so than a simple cheerleader, who usually wears a plain cotton uniform (except for NFL cheerleaders, but that's misusing the power of sparkles if you ask me). Hairpieces are often used to achieve coordinating poufs among the twirl line and lipstick is custom ordered to harmonize with the sequins.

After a few years, someone hurt my feelings and broke the news to me that I was skinny, so when it came time for high school and Daddy asked if I wanted to audition for majorette, I replied, "Humph! That's for girls who can't read music." I had moved on to another silver love, the flute, but would never confess the real reason for shunning the majorette gig was because even in the sweltering Southern month of September, I felt much more secure beneath the cover of a heavy wool band uniform than a skimpy costume, no matter how many rhinestones they tried to bribe me with.

In college, my roommate was a former all-star twirler from her high school, but in those days, the universities had the gall to enforce weight and height restrictions, and since she was a curvaceous five-foot, one-inch beauty, she didn't even bother. But she brought her bag of batons with her to school, and she and I would stand on the front lawn of the dorm and twirl and spin until we had a group of girls join us, all laughing and shouting at the fun. It seemed like we all had a smidgen of inner majorette just dying to get out.

The most incredible twirling feat I've ever witnessed came from two male twirlers at Troy University. Each young man stood in an end zone and at the given moment threw their batons across the entire length of the field to each other, over the head of an Elvis impersonator who was playing an electric guitar on the 50-yard line, and then to the crowd's delight . . . caught them! No one remembered what song Elvis was playing, but we all went home talking about the magnificent majorettes . . . uh . . . majors . . . baton twirlers.

This year, when it came time for the Christmas parade, I stood in front of the hardware store and heard the sound of drums approaching. And I swanee, if not one, not two, but three entire groups of baton twirlers came strutting down Fairhope Avenue! Adorable babes and girls ready for the big leagues were all sparkles and smiles. Hallelujah! You just wait and see. Civility will once again rule the earth, puppies will smell sweeter, and a Southerner will reclaim the title of Miss America. All in the world will be right again, because the majorettes are back in town.

# Humidity Threatens Our Crowning Glory

There are three things Southern women take very seriously: God, family, and their hair. And we all know God and our families want us to have pretty hair. I seem to recall a Bible verse that said, "The bigger the hair, the closer to God," or is it something about a "crowning glory?"

So, my theological conundrum is this: if God loves Southerners enough to give us okra, grits, and college football and tells the ladies that our hair is our crowning glory, then why on His green earth would God send the South so much humidity?

Although we love to have big, poufy hair, *à la* Miss Watermelon Queen 1989, we also want it to be sleek, smooth, and shiny. But the same humidity that people swear is the secret to our dewy, glowing skin is also a major enemy to the perfectly coiffed look. Muggy air produces frizz, and frizz is the wrong kind of big.

To add insult to injury, just when we think we've found the perfect products from Bee-Bee's Beauty Barn that promise to battle the humidity, age jumps into the game and wrecks our 'dos. In all the books I found slid under my childhood door about our "changing bodies," none of them mentioned the horror of having my hair's texture transform as I grew older. Combined with humidity, my "maturing" hair doesn't stand a chance.

When my beach vacation was interrupted with three days of steamy tropical rain, I discovered my hair was reverting to my three-year-old little girl style and crimped to the point of being curly. So now it's easier to have curls in the hot months than my desired sleek look of the South. It's more of a "wild woman" look than "proper Southern lady," and although I'm not a big fan of the curls, for some reason, my husband loves it.

When the season arrives for us to put away the seersucker and pull out the team jersey, we know the soggy days of humidity are on their way out. Ladies who have been hiding beneath hats, ponytails, and a croaker sack full of barrettes, headbands, and pins are suddenly freed from oppression and are able to once again sport the smooth, flowing, poufy hair belles were meant to have. Barbie dolls have nothing on us when it comes to a crisp autumn day. By mid-October, Southern belles finally get to "let their hair down" in the truest sense.

Maybe God gives the Southern states so much humidity so we won't take pretty hair for granted. People in other areas of the country don't seem to care nearly as much about how their hair looks and often wear what they call "practical" styles (whatever that means).

I learned dry air is our hair's best friend while on a trip to Arizona and had my all-time best hair day ever. The Grand Canyon crowd was very impressed with my big, Southern hairdo. Thanks to the dry heat, my hair stayed perfectly smooth and poufy all day long.

Come to think of it, you would think there would be more Miss Americas from the Midwest, seeing how they have the non-humidity advantage. If you will recall, the best Miss America ever, Alabama's own Heather Whitestone, almost always had to wear her hair pulled back. Even our homegrown royalty wasn't exempt from the menacing muggy air, but clever Heather discovered that firmly securing her hair with a sparkling crown is the best solution of all and like many other belles took it to heart that hair is truly our "crowning" glory.

# Decoration...Not Just for Cakes

Decoration isn't always something you put on a cake. In the South, there remain pockets of small communities that celebrate Decoration Day. Those who observe this occasion usually refer to it simply as "Decoration." I grew up thinking everyone went to Decoration and was amazed to discover it's observed in only a few Southern communities.

My mother's family in North Alabama observes Decoration, but my father's family in North Florida had never heard of it. Some friends in South Carolina go to Decoration, but no one I know in Georgia has any idea what it's about.

My father was a little stunned when he realized that once a year he would be required to put on his best suit and go stand around in the cemetery with his in-laws, both the living and the dearly departed. That's basically what it is: standing around, admiring the graves, and remembering those gone on before us (to heaven, not to the Golden Corral).

Decoration isn't the same as Memorial Day; that's for our armed forces. Some say Memorial Day actually grew out of Confederate Memorial Day, which is believed to have originated with regular, old-fashioned Decoration Day. This is why Decoration celebrations are often found in older, more historic communities where little has changed over the years.

In the few areas that still celebrate Decoration, people go all out. Signs on businesses announce, "Get your

Decoration chicken bucket here!" or "Decoration Sale—turnips half price." This year, my mother's hometown of Hartselle even had the big-box store get in on the act by stocking a huge selection of Decoration grave flowers, as if the local florists haven't been holding their own all these years.

What keeps Decoration even more underground (oh, now there's the pun of the century) is the fact that each community observes Decoration on a different day of the year. Hartselle celebrates the occasion on Mother's Day.

Several carloads of various relatives arrive at the cemetery on what I guess would be Decoration Eve and, using whisk brooms, hand shovels, and clippers, clean the graves of all our relatives. After all plots are neat and tidy, we place flower arrangements on the headstones.

On Sunday morning, we dress in our best. I always recycle my Easter dress from a few weeks before, then proceed to the cemetery, where we meander throughout the hillside graves, admiring the mounds of beautiful flowers and chatting with the other families who have also spent the previous day decorating their loved ones' resting places. It's a given that we will stop to admire the ancient Indian burial sites where stones have been neatly stacked on top for ages. No one dares touch them out of reverence and a healthy dose of fear left over from childhood stories.

There's something about standing in a plot that bears your name, literally carved in stone, at a time when you aren't consumed with grief from an actual funeral that is peaceful and sweet. You tend to reflect kindly on those buried and think about how they would have loved seeing how everyone has grown and changed. One year, my boys skipped around the graves in their little seersucker suits and as I started to tell them to stop, something told me my grandfather, who they happened to be hopping over, would have told me to leave them alone and let them play. "They're just being little boys," I heard his voice say. Remembering what our loved ones were like is exactly why we're there.

The day used to end with dinner on the grounds beneath the large oaks, but it's been relocated in recent years to a home with the promise of shelter from the elements and comfortable chairs for the older folks.

Decoration keeps us tied to "our people." It's a tradition that keeps us—oh, I can't say it—grounded. Just like Scarlett had a passionate longing to return to Tara, we too understand the pull of home, even if no kinfolk remain.

Even though we're a mobile society that has moved away from the places where generations before have called home, we still return and fulfill the duties of Decoration. We pull weeds from headstones, prepare plates of deviled eggs and gallon jugs of tea, then dress up and stand at footstones to listen while older folks tell of long-ago memories. We pass around babies, give hugs, and promise to return the next year, never knowing who will be the one to decorate or be decorated.

# Don't Throw Your Pearls before Wine

I swanee! My pearls broke and bounced all over tarnation and now I'm about to lose my mind trying to find them all. It wasn't my everyday short strand I wear around the house; instead, it was the longer one inherited from my Great-Aunt Vina Mae.

When Vina Mae passed away with no children of her own, the eligible cousins (those not living in the "gated community" in Atmore) gathered at her house and spread her valuable mementoes on the dining room table then took turns selecting a few items we liked as a way to remember our dearly departed aunt.

Cousin John-Jack went first and chose a Case pocket knife left in our aunt's care by a long-forgotten yet scandalous beau, then cousin Rosie Belle from Robertsdale got the next pick. I tried to give her the subliminal message, "Don't pick the pearls; don't pick the pearls!" I guess the message got through, because she chose a pretty emerald ring she now wears to her traditional worship service and admires as it sparkles when she holds her hymnal in the stained-glass-infused sunbeam.

My turn was next, and although Aunt Vina Mae's cast-iron skillet collection was tempting—and yes, as many of you understand, we consider the perfectly seasoned cast iron to be part of the "valuables"—I still pounced on the pearls. They had an appealing warm, creamy glow, the color of hot grits or a fragrant magnolia, and also carried the deeply sentimental memory of my aunt wearing them when we would go shopping at Maison Morgan in Hartselle.

I'd been wearing Auntie's pearls for about a year and in the back of my mind knew I should have them restrung because the knots in between the pearls had worn smooth, but I put it off, and now I'm sorry.

Since I had a day full of festive events, beginning with the customer appreciation sale at Talbot's, then lunch with the art guild ladies, and ending with an executive board meeting for the Committee for the Preservation of Loveliness, I decided Auntie's longer strand was more appropriate. In between my very important appointments, I also had to run to the Piggly Wiggly to restock my standard staples of the red, white, and blue (red wine, White Lily flour, and Blue Bell ice cream).

As I rushed around the kitchen throwing everything into place, I took care to hide the wine because my party-girl neighbor, Donna Jean, called to say she was on her way over to return my Pyrex I'd left with her the week before when I delivered a casserole to her house (her entire family had the crud). I knew if she saw the merlot, she'd want to sit and have a glass (or two), which would make me late for my last meeting. But when I twirled my pearls out of the way, they somehow became entangled with the neck of the bottle of merlot, and the next thing I knew, tiny flecks of white were flying through the air like a dandelion scattered in the wind.

The popping sound was like a shot through my heart. I didn't realize pearls were so bouncy and as they scattered, I tried to shoo away my beagle, Lois Lane, who immediately thought they were treats. Beagles think everything that hits the floor is delicious manna from God.

An ocean of pearls swirled beneath my feet, around the furniture, and everywhere I looked. If it wasn't so tragic, it would have been beautiful.

I'm currently keeping the loose pearls in an old Cool Whip bowl until they can be taken to the jeweler. But I'm not ready to take them just yet, because every time I walk through the room, I spy another tiny white orb hiding here or there, and I want to wait until I've located every single one (minus the two devoured by Lois Lane).

All of this pearly trauma has taught me a very important lesson: take care of your nice things, both pearls and friends. If your neighbor wants a glass of wine, slow down and let her have it. Savor your relationships. Pearls are precious, but life is short, so take a deep breath, be a good hostess, and no matter what, never cast your pearls before wine.

# Mimi and the Southern Zucchini

Cousin Rosie Belle from Robertsdale just stopped by with an old Piggly Wiggly bag full of good things from her garden: mostly squash, a few tomatoes, and just enough new potatoes for my dinner. I sent her home with bunches of herbs and a bouquet of zinnias.

Southerners are the givin'est bunch of people you'll ever meet. Anytime we visit one another, we always want to "take a little something." And even though the "little" is often quite small, it's truly the thought that counts. Unless, of course, it's zucchini.

No one wants to look out their window and see you coming down the drive with a mess of the overplanted, overabundant, and greatly underused squash. You know the saying, "The only time we have to lock our car doors around here is late summer, to keep people from slipping zucchini onto the backseat." There's an actual "National Sneak Some Zucchini onto Your Neighbor's Porch Day," which is observed August 8, although here in Alabama, zucchini season comes early and we start piling up the abundant vegetable in July. Why we plant so much when we know we can't possibly eat it all is just another quirk in our long line of agricultural heritage. It's like being able to name and cook 453 dishes that come from a pig. It's just something ingrained in our DNA.

Zucchini is a fine, if not tasty vegetable, but when you feel obligated to cook it forty times a week—because we've also been taught by our frugal ancestors not to waste anything for fear of slipping into another Great Depression and having to go to work for the TVA—it becomes a heavy burden.

The summer of '84 was a particularly prolific year for zucchini. Mama used it in stews, casseroles, and salads and since it stood still for more than thirty seconds, she also fried it. After Daddy brought yet another heaping bucket of zucchini in from the garden, Mama then resorted to baking zucchini cookies. It was at that moment we realized that she secretly hated us.

"Fine. Be that way then. If you don't want to eat the zucchini that your Daddy worked so hard to grow (Hard? It's like kudzu. You just think about it and it comes up.), then take some over to Miss Melba Jean's house. I'm sure her children will appreciate it."

"No, Mom. You forgot we already took them zucchini last week, and I think they're actually the ones who retaliated and snuck some of their zucchini onto our porch last night."

But of all the people to become unhinged over the gift of garden bounty, the most memorable was my husband's grandmother, Mimi, who moved to Alabama to be near us in her later years. Having been born and raised in New York City for the first part of her life, and then relocating to the NYC suburb of Boynton Beach, Florida, Mimi was unaccustomed to our Southern ways.

First of all, Mimi was amazed that everyone she met in Alabama had the same speech impediment I did. For years she couldn't understand a word I said, and she finally figured out why.

Mimi's formal and somewhat stoic ways were tested time and again when total strangers would try to start up a conversation with her. At first she thought I knew everyone in town, but she then realized we just talk to everyone.

Mimi learned that in a long line, people in Alabama could make a new friend, swap a recipe, and get witnessed to, all before they reach the register. The poor woman was terrified.

Another thing that required some adjustment was Mimi's extreme vigilance of her pocketbook. Always wary due to her New York street smarts, she'd clutch her purse to her chest through an entire movie or somehow wrap it around an arm or a leg throughout dinner in a restaurant. When she accompanied us to our church's Wednesday night dinner, I tried to get her to leave her purse at the table while we went through the serving line, but the streetwise New Yorker cleverly balanced her plate atop the bulging bag and put dessert in the other hand.

So, when zucchini season rolled around, we weren't surprised when after we'd taken her to lunch, she held her pocketbook firm as we walked her to her door and found a recycled grocery bag full of fresh vegetables from someone's garden hanging on her doorknob. Suddenly outraged, the great-grandmother exclaimed, "Can you believe someone would think I need their old, discarded food?" Mimi truly felt humiliated and offended that someone had offered her charity. "And on top of that," she added, "you just don't know where this food has been. Anyone could slip something into it." Mimi was always mindful of the razorblade-in-the-apple story from Halloween.

After looking through the bag that Mimi had flung on the kitchen counter, I found two ripe tomatoes, a bell pepper, and enough zucchini for a week of suppers. I explained the best I could that this was probably a gift from a neighbor or church member who had stopped by to check on her. It was a sign of friendship and neighborliness, not a handout.

The most puzzled and confused look came over her face, and then it was just like New York snow melting in the warm sun of the South. A small grin appeared on her face and Mimi's heart grew three times that day as she learned the agricultural lesson of Southern hospitality at its finest.

We never discovered who left the gift for Mimi that day, and little did they know that in addition to planting vegetables, they also planted the seeds of friendship, trust, and kindness. And a new variety of transplanted Southern belle began to grow, faster and far more prolific than any zucchini I've ever seen.

# Our Simple Southern Home

*"Our Simple Southern Home" touched many readers upon its original publication and inspired them to send me notes telling of their own ways they celebrate the simplicity of the rural South. From spending time at a favorite grandparent's house with no TV or internet and only the field or forest to play in and explore or drifting on a small boat in a lake with childhood friends, all our sweet memories of happiness tend to come from basic activities that children today seem to miss.*

*Computers and all the other blinking gadgets that go with them don't compare to the fun that can be found in an afternoon with those we love, laughing and talking on the old front porch swing.*

*The South was grown from simple times, simple food, and simple customs. To abandon those ways now seems exciting to some, but even with all our technology and busy schedules, there's a longing to return to Southern simplicity.*

Although our world seems to be thrilled with the excitement of fast food, instant information, and abbreviated conversations, some of us still understand that happiness often springs from the simple, slow, and easy things in life.

Now, a study from the University of Chicago confirms this notion and has "discovered" what Southerners could have told them a long time ago. The earth-shaking research concluded that true, bonafide happiness doesn't come from the big, thrilling events in our lives but instead stems from the simple, ordinary moments in our regular, hum-drum days.

And everyone in Mayberry said, "No duh."

The academic study revealed that although people like to experience short-lived excitement like jumping out of an airplane or seeing an opening night Broadway show (I'll take the show), true happiness and the best memories in life are found by leaping from a rope swing into the cold creek with a group of friends on a hot summer afternoon or seeing a "show" performed by the children in the church fellowship hall. Boring to some city slickers, but those of us raised on grits fully comprehend the joys of simplicity.

Although there are those in the South who have begun to assimilate with the rest of the country when it comes to living in the fast lane with a constant need to be entertained, most of us still know how to take it easy and are happiest when using old-fashioned face-to-face conversation. We've found something gets lost if we try to text a Jerry Clower joke, and anyway, no one is completely sure just how to spell "OOooo-weeee!"

The simple style of our lives may also be related in part to economics. Since our region ranks lower on the national income level, we may not have as many opportunities for big adventure. At the same time, Southerners also rank highest in charitable giving—because helping our neighbors is another simple thing that makes us incredibly happy.

Our penchant for the easy life may also be related to Dixie's milder climate. Being able to get out of the house and swing beneath the giant live oak for the better part of the year gives us time to decompress and value the simplistic beauty of nature instead of being trapped indoors with contraptions that beep and flash.

If I close my eyes and think of all the exciting places I've been and the excellent, fancy meals I've eaten, the happiest dinner I remember was the simplest of all. Weary of a long, hot summer packed with a series of stressful events, I decided to shake things up. I bypassed the regular kitchen and dining room tables and instead unfolded the small gate-legged table in the living room and pulled it up to the fireplace to use the hearth as a bench seat. A roundup of a couple of wayward chairs, a poufy ottoman, and mismatched dinnerware on the table was all anchored by a centerpiece of pretty weeds and a half-burned Halloween candle. I pulled out all the leftovers from the refrigerator and created a mishmash of food that would have earned me a failing grade in any home economics class. I called my family into the room and told them we were having a "crazy supper," and they had sixty seconds to run around the house, find a costume, and return to their seats.

We sat around the table that night with two little boys laughing hysterically, wearing hats, inside-out shirts, and flowing superhero capes, eating a scrumptious yet strange supper of cold spaghetti, meatloaf, pickled okra, and pimento cheese. As Louis Armstrong serenaded us in the background, my husband looked at me through his Batman mask, and we knew we had found deep and memorable happiness through an easy dinner of simple leftovers.

So, go ahead and search for happiness by running with the bulls, swimming with the sharks, or climbing a mountain. Southerners don't need a university study to tell us these kinds of things only bring temporary joy because we've always known the greatest happiness is found upon returning home from our adventures to find our dog wagging his tail on the front porch of our very happy, yet simple Southern home.

# The Bigger the Bow, the More Mama Loves You

If our hair is our crowning glory, then a big, fluffy hair bow is the jewel in the crown of all little girls in the South. Boiled down to the bare-bones truth, a hair bow represents how much love a mama has for her precious, darlin' lamb. Matching every outfit, with special editions for each holiday, a poufy bow adds an extra touch of cuteness to an already adorable child. Even if the little belle loves to play sports, the bow will always be there, coordinating with the uniform and often monogramed with the team logo.

I thought little girls everywhere wore hair bows, but a friend new to our area of Alabama who has never lived in the South was both amazed and in somewhat of a panic when she asked, "Where do I find these hair bows? My daughter suddenly has to have some to fit in with the other girls in Miss Penelope's Preschool Ponderosa."

Having only boys, I had no idea what to tell her about finding big, bodacious bows. They seem like such a natural piece of the puzzle, I always assumed the accessory came with the pink-swaddled baby the day she was brought home from the hospital.

My own childhood hair bows somehow automatically showed up on my head and I never thought about how they got there. Back in the days when I didn't have enough hair to hold a clip, and you couldn't buy Velcro (at least not in Florala), Mama resorted to Scotch Tape to hold the mandatory accessory neatly in place, which taught me lesson number 24 in the Southern belle playbook: it's better to look good than to feel good.

I asked around, and one friend told me that when her daughter was in first grade, she had more than fifty different bows, with twelve of those having a specific Christmas theme. Looking into space and tapping on her fingers, she recited, "There was the reindeer bow, the snowman bow, the Wise Men bow, and of course, her favorite, the angel bow, which had little silver bells sewn in."

One thing all my girlfriends agree on is that if you have a daughter who refuses to wear a hair bow when she's a tot, then you had better lock her up now, because those are the babes who grow up to be wild women. I remember reading somewhere that scientists at the University of South Alabama found a direct correlation between girls who reject childhood hair bows and those who grow up to dance on tables at the Flora-Bama.

After little girls outgrow the regular, daily hair bows, they move into the teenage years when cheerleaders and the all-American majorettes sport the team-colored hair accessories with their names monogramed on the edges. "Olivia," "Alivia," and "Oliveeah" all flip and march across the field with their beautiful bows bouncing and make their mamas' hearts swell with pride.

But the real reason we place beautiful bows on the heads of our precious girls is to prepare them for the ultimate crowning glory: tiaras. If your head is accustomed to holding a bow, then you instinctively know how to rock a row of rhinestones.

Later, we advance to pretty hats, which aren't as bouncy as bows nor as sparkly as tiaras but still great fun to wear. Popping on a pretty hat in the South is not only stylish, it also has the added benefit of taming the gosh-awful, humidity-induced frizz which is our one and only curse for living in a place otherwise considered paradise (if you don't count the mosquitoes and hurricanes).

I can only hope and pray my boys will someday marry young ladies who were blessed to have worn big, fat, fluffy hair bows as little girls. But if these girls tell me they didn't like wearing bows . . . well, let's just say we won't be dining at the Flora-Bama any time soon.

# Just Charming

I need to discuss something with you," my mother said in her very serious mom-voice. She had called that afternoon, and knowing how she always tries to brace me for bad news with a lead-in statement, I prepared myself for something dreadful. "I want to give you my charm bracelet."

"Oh, dear God. She's dying," I thought. Next to her wedding rings, my mother has always loved her charm bracelet more than any other piece of jewelry. She started collecting the gold charms for her heavy bracelet when she was a freshman at Howard College, now Samford University, where my son is currently a student. The cherished bracelet is loaded with jingles and jangles from decades of happy memories and special events, and after she assured me she was in great health, my second completely human and natural yet competitive thought was, "If I'm getting the bracelet, then what are they giving my brother? Aww, who cares? I'm getting the charm bracelet!"

I think my parents have reached the point in their lives where it's practical to clear out the unused things around the house. They're tired of the excess and want to simplify and organize. They love to travel, and I think Mama is tired of hiding things like her charm bracelet in the bread box every time they leave town.

She explained, "I've just decided that I've worn it enough and I think you would enjoy it more, so I want to go ahead and give it to you now rather than later." And you know, she's right. I was jumping up and down, excited to get the bracelet, which features a little bride charm along with class rings that belonged to her and my father.

I remember sitting in church on Sunday nights (she was in the choir loft in the morning service) and playing ever so quietly with each charm. I'd examine the bridesmaid holding a bouquet, the bulldog pup, and the two children—one for me, one for my brother. I'd slowly turn the bracelet around her arm to examine the tiny engagement ring and the "Merry Christmas" tree on the other side.

Charm bracelets were all the rage in the 1950s and have remained popular in the South, where belles have always had a passion for beautiful, sparkly things. Charms have made a recent comeback in the fashion world and ladies around the country are creating new bracelets for themselves as well as hunting down older, antique charms due to their detail and uniqueness.

The bracelet never fails to attract someone who comments on it and then shares her own bracelet story. It's a sorority of sorts, with a charming bond where we share details of our collections with our heads close together as if we are examining a golden scrapbook.

My mother was wise in knowing I would treasure her bobbling bijoux bangle, and she has delighted in seeing tokens of her fondest memories dangle from my wrist. Not only do I know her bracelet, I know her stories.

Even though he's a teenage boy, my own son sometimes reaches over in church and pokes his fingers around the charms. "I like the bulldog best," he whispers. Maybe the family bracelet will be the ultimate test to see if his future wife is worthy. ("Oh, I don't like charm bracelets, they're too noisy"—she's out. "Oh, I adore your bracelet!"—she's a keeper.)

As for my brother, he was excited to be given a large set of tools, which was completely fine with me. There would be nothing charming at all about a wrench dangling from my dainty wrist, now would there? Oh, how our charming parents know us so well.

# The Best Halftime Show Ever

My only involvement in the best halftime show ever was donating my lunch money towards the purchase of the pig. Other than that, I was a completely innocent freshman.

Our football team at Escambia High School was having a few rough years, but our band was awesome. Our nemesis, Tate High School, battled us for top spot at all the local band contests. They considered their stiff military style to be far superior to our laid-back, fun shows. Tate sneered at our old uniforms, laughed at our band room's lack of air conditioning, and then called our mamas names. Whereas their director was more John Philip Sousa, ours was Jimmy Buffett, and they hated us for our casual attitude. The insults and pranks between the bands reached new heights when Tate selected us as their homecoming opponent. Everyone knew they had chosen us because they considered our team to be a patsy.

After we perfected the most awesome halftime show ever known to man, Tate informed us we would have to perform before the game began because they wanted the entire halftime for themselves. Of all the low-down nerve! No one would even see our show. The crowd would still be trickling into the stands while we played our hearts out. That's when the plan was hatched by the senior trumpet player, who winked at me as I handed him my $1.10.

Even though the score was sure to be lopsided, it was the game of the week and broadcast on live TV. We performed our show to the predicted empty stands then settled in to watch the butt-kicking take place. Tate's band played their irritating fight song over and over after every touchdown as their students laughed and pointed at us from across the field.

At halftime, the Pride of Cantonment marched onto the field and launched into "Ice Castles" as their polyester-clad homecoming court sashayed down the 50-yard line on the arms of their cousins.

Operation "Old McDonald" began to unfold with a precision only known to our hometown Blue Angels. Our mastermind innocently walked beneath the stands carrying a sousaphone case. Hidden below us, he pushed out the metal air grate at the front of the cement bleachers facing the field and opened the case to release a medium-sized pink pig, which cost $62.47.

Pigs have worked for Hollywood and not performed as well. He obediently started at one end zone, ran cattywampus through the legs of Tate's band members, knocked over a couple of color guard girls, then triumphantly relieved himself on the 50-yard line in front of the newly crowned queen.

By this time, the crowd had begun to whoop and holler. Three sturdy boys from Tate's FFA gave chase and added to the commotion by diving in and out of the band, taking out a ticked-off saxophone player. The announcer didn't know what to do other than say, "Folks, I think we have a pig on the field."

Piggy ran on, free and unscathed, through the band as "Ice Castles" fell apart, and when he crossed into the far end zone, the crowd yelled, "Touchdown!" Girls with corsages cried, their band director cursed, and the TV cameras captured it all for the viewers at home.

Our director and principal looked away to hide their laughter. It was still the era when no one was suspended or sent to juvenile detention and PETA didn't get their britches in a bunch. Tate students took it as a new opportunity to hate us even more, but decades later, they got the last laugh.

The last time I checked, the odiferous paper mill looming over the school had been updated, property values soared, and kids from my school grew up, moved north, and enrolled their offspring in Tate. And although I've called them traitors to their faces, they assure me that each time they sit in that stadium and watch their children wear Tate's crimson and gray, they hum a few notes of "Old McDonald" and think of the best halftime show ever.

# To Think That It Started with a Tiny Boll Weevil

With a slow drawl, the lion keeper at the University of North Alabama said, "You can't claim to be a true Alabamian until you've been to the National Peanut Festival in Dothan," so Hoss King, who was a senior oboe major, grabbed his roommate, Billy Mac, and took off to celebrate the famous legume. After a quick stop in Cullman to say "hey" to Hoss's mama, who fed them pimento cheese sandwiches and pickled okra, the boys continued south until they came to Houston County, where they promptly ran out of gas.

After they had walked a couple of miles, a blue Honda Civic carrying two young ladies pulled up and offered the college boys a ride. Of all things, the girls, with pink foam rollers in their hair, were on their way to the Miss Peanut pageant as contestants. "It isn't all about beauty, you know," said the pretty driver, Patty Sue. "We're quizzed on everything there is to know about peanuts. For instance, did you know that half of all peanuts produced in the United States are grown within a hundred-mile radius of Dothan?"

Not to be outdone, the girl in the passenger seat chimed in, "And did you know arachibutyrophobia is the fear of getting peanut butter stuck to the roof of your mouth?" Then the girl laughed so hard, the boys noticed she looked like she had plowed up an entire field of peanuts with her two front teeth. Bless her heart.

By the time they'd reached the gas station and after hearing all the chatter about peanuts, Billy Mac felt like he'd hitched a ride with Dr. George Washington Carver himself. But Hoss was totally smitten with Patty Sue, and that night at the pageant, he sat in the front row and cheered wildly when she won the peanut crown. The determined oboist spent the next semester burning up the roads from the northwest part of the state to the southeast corner to win the hand of the royal Peanut Queen herself, pretty Patty Sue.

The two lovebirds went on to marry and served salty peanuts, ready to pour into cold, fizzy, glass bottles of Co-Cola at their wedding. Over the years, Mr. and Mrs. King had four children of their own: Pickles, Pepper, and Peaches, all girls, and finally a son, appropriately given the real-life legal name of Peanut King. Little Peanut King was a popular fellow in school where the family settled on the outskirts of Dothan and had enough land to grow a small peanut patch of their own.

The dirty, rotten, low-down boll weevil that destroyed the cotton crops in South Alabama so many years ago was heralded as an unlikely hero for forcing the farmers to switch their crops to peanuts, therefore reinvigorating the local economy and saving many farms. A much-larger-than-life statue of the nefarious critter was placed in the center of nearby Enterprise as a warning to other varmints not to mess with Alabama farmers.

Just like Joseph in the Bible, who was sold into slavery by his good-for-nothin' brothers, what started out as evil (rhymes with "weevil." Coincidence? I think not.) turned into something good. Kind of like running out of gas all those years ago helped Hoss King to unite in holy matrimony with the Peanut Queen and become the daddy of little Peanut King, who is now grown and following in his daddy's footsteps by playing second-chair oboe in the Birmingham symphony.

The pastors in Wiregrass Country remain fond of reminding us, "What you meant for evil, God meant for good." Or as they say in Dothan, "To think, it all started with a tiny boll weevil."

# The Cruelest Month of All

With apologies to T.S. Eliot and his long—very long poem—*The Waste Land,* I must take exception to his proclamation that "April is the cruelest month." Obviously, Eliot never tried to properly dress nor accessorize himself during a sultry Southern September.

On one hand, September is a beautiful, fun-filled month with end-of-summer parties and back-to-school sales. But for some reason, society throws cold water on our fun and insists we shortchange summer and begin autumn the second we turn the page on the calendar. Don't they know? September is definitely still summer in the South.

You see, we want to act like it's fall. We want the hay rides, pumpkins, and Halloween decorations, but in the South, it's still just too blame hot to even pretend autumn is anywhere near.

Northern regions start to feel a nip in the air sometimes as early as late August, and they begin tossing pumpkins and scarecrows around with little attention to the calendar at all. They don't care about hurting our feelings, and they start wearing beautiful earth-toned sweaters and scarves. You can still smell the Labor Day burgers in the air here, while people "up there" begin tossing cozy blankets by the fireplace and snuggling with their furry dogs. We'd never be jealous or envy them one minute, except with the invention of Pinterest, Instagram, and Facebook, we're bombarded with their photos of nippy nights by a bonfire and chilly mornings sipping hot chocolate while we're still drenched in humidity and battling mosquitoes.

Sure, we still have the beach, which is a big plus for Team South, but by September, we're ready for a change and feel just a little envious watching the Yankees play outdoors without breaking a sweat.

Southern Septembers are tricky. The ninth month of the year still looks, feels, smells, and sounds like summer to us. Our silver bowl of seashells remains on the coffee table, and our beach chairs are still in the back of the sandy car. Jimmy Buffett tunes continue to run through our heads, and while we lounge at the beach, we flip through magazines that tease us with cutie-pie fall wreaths made from leaves with colors unlike anything we've ever seen in our own yards.

We want to wear sweaters but faint at the thought. We want to simmer stews on the stove, but they'd go uneaten. We want to throw open the windows and have crisp breezes tickle the curtains, but to survive, we'd have to run the air conditioner nonstop.

While the Northerners are snickering at our lack of hot tea savvy, we have to act like we know what a real autumn looks like by purchasing plastic pumpkins that won't rot and not wearing white or seersucker after Labor Day. I personally feel the wearing of white should be extended to the official end of summer and not end at Labor Day, but who am I to change the rotation of the world? If I wore white shoes after Labor Day, the Southern fashion police would throw the book at me, and that's a painful punishment not understood by any Northerner.

For us, getting dressed in September is downright confusing. We want to look fall-ish, but boots and sweaters send us into heat stroke. I'm slightly more sympathetic than I once was and have stopped thumping strangers on the nose for wearing white shorts and sandals in

September, even if they deserve it. I figure the stares and murmured comments from every Southern belle they pass are punishment enough. But my heart goes out to them, because it's too early for winter white wools but too late for bright white. Is it just the shoes, or do the rules apply to other clothing as well? Oh, the agony!

Open-toed sandals are okay in rich fall tones like brown or black, but flip-flops . . . Oh, mercy daisy. Toe-spreading, sole-slapping footwear is a trend only outdone by rubbery clown-colored Crocs. Let's just say, "Oh Vinetta, those glued-on rhinestones make your flip-flops look so fancy!" is a sentence that is incorrect on many, many levels, in any state of the union, any month of the year.

So, for now, fellow Southerners, we're resigned to spend September tracking oncoming hurricanes while dressed in our own interpretation of autumn fashion, which ends up being a lightweight brown T-shirt, tan shorts, and brown sandals. We'll sip our pumpkin-spiced lattes over ice and put plastic leaf wreaths on our doors that won't go limp in the heat. We'll watch football in our air-conditioned homes and use the garden hose to simultaneously perk up our wilting flowers and wash the love bugs off the car grill.

Ahh, September. If not the coolest, then the cruelest month of all, y'all.

# Southern Ladylike Words

Everyone knows Southerners have their own charming language. From the melodic pronunciation of the words to the cleverly worded meanings, we manage to say what we mean and mean what we say, and it makes no difference if outsiders understand us or not. We have the ability to tell you off and have you beg us to tell you again.

Southern ladies in particular have accumulated a language that harkens back to the olden days, mainly because our families are so important to us that we grew up sitting at the feet of our grandmothers and great-aunts as they visited on the front porch. What better place to learn the lessons of life?

Here is my list of a few of my favorite ladylike Southern words. I can almost hear Great-Aunt Petunia Mae saying them now.

Warning: Use sparingly, or you'll overwhelm the person to whom you are speaking. Bless their heart.

| | |
|---|---|
| Lovely | Kinfolk |
| Precious | Spartan |
| Cherish | Yearn |
| Darling | Pocketbook |
| Skedaddle | Dashing |
| Fetching | Contemplate |
| Adorable | Sweetie |
| Flawless | Beau |

Hooligan
Gumption
Sugar/Honey
Bonafide
Soirée
Divine
Delightful
Charming
Loath
Dandy
Cad

Sparkle
Consume
Imbibe
Embellish
Enchanting
Drudgery
Peckish
Honorable
Deranged
Striking
Elegant

And where would we be without the ever-needed "tacky?"

# II.
## Our Precious Southern Families

O h, how we love our families in the South. Of course, "love" can also mean "tolerate." We're big, loud, and loyal, and as my grandparents would say when they hugged me, "She's a good girl, for the shape she's in." Which meant, "We love you the way you are." We tend to be strict with our children, kind to our pets, and flirty with our spouse. It makes life easier to know everyone's behaving as they should.

# The Worst Valentine's Day Gift Ever

This year, my husband and I celebrated Valentine's Day like a boring mom and dad instead of dreamy-eyed lovers. Earlier that day, our son had his wisdom teeth extracted, so we spent the evening dishing out ice cream and keeping him off social media. There's nothing worse than a woozy, tipsy teen who thinks it's a good idea to post updates on Instagram.

But no matter how mundane the celebration, it was still better than the year I gave my husband, Bob, the absolute worst Valentine's Day gift ever.

After a few unusually stressful months of crazy schedules, I realized Valentine's Day was approaching and decided to surprise my husband with something we could both enjoy. See what I did there? I played the game of getting a gift for "him" but making sure it was something I'd like too.

A local resort had just opened a beautiful spa that was advertising a special Valentine's Day romantic couple's massage. Complete with champagne, flowers, and chocolate, we could relax and enjoy a soothing massage together. No Nerf gun wars, barking dogs, or dirty kitchens— just the two of us on a self-indulgent, relaxing date. What could go wrong?

I made the reservation and surprised Bob with the news. Less than enthused, he complained, "That sounds weird. I don't want to go." I told him, "We deserve to be pampered and I promise you'll love it!"

I finally convinced him (the non-refundable deposit worked in my favor), and off we went for our romantic adventure. With the lights low and soothing sounds of the rainforest coming from the Bose speaker, we slipped onto the tables, just a few feet from each other, and waited. Ahh . . . I could already feel the stress melting away. The door opened and a nice lady in her mid-fifties introduced herself and said she'd be giving me my massage. As she lit a fabulous-smelling candle, the door opened again and Bob's masseuse arrived.

With a melodic foreign accent, she said, "Hello, I'm Katarina and I'll be your masseuse." Katarina was six feet tall, blonde, and had just defected from the Swedish Bikini Team. The super-girl couldn't have been a day over twenty-five and smelled like coconuts. I didn't understand how she possibly could have sufficient hand coordination to give a proper massage, since she obviously had trouble buttoning her blouse.

My husband looked over at me with a big smile and said, "You were so right. I'm going to love this. I should listen to you more often."

My eyes popped wide open and there was absolutely no relaxing on my side of the room. "Wow, you are really tense," commented my masseuse. But I could barely hear her from all the noise coming from the other side of the room: "Mmmm! Ahh! OH YES!"

As the two women turned to get more magic potions, lotions, or whatever it was that was supposed to make us happy, I whispered, "Dang it (then said his full baptism name), you stop that right now!"

"What?"

"You know what I mean. Stop enjoying yourself so much!"

"But . . . I thought that's what you wanted me to do!"

"You know exactly what I mean."

My dearest lay there on the table looking like a crayon in the August sun and smiled as Katarina (if that was even her real name) returned and slowly kneaded his shoulders. I thought I heard purring.

I was like a prairie dog whose head kept popping up to look around. What? Hey! Huh? The tension was thick, at least on my side of the room.

Never had I wanted a massage to end more than I did right then. "Time's up? Oh, what a pity. Come on, darling, let's get out of here."

Sounding like he had a mouth full of gravel, Bob said, "I don't think I can ever move again, I'm so relaxed. It's like a drug, you know."

"Well, people get arrested for doing drugs, and Jesus doesn't look favorably on it either, so let's get out of here."

After that Valentine's Day experience, taking care of a groggy teenager was downright romantic.

# Baby Buford Doesn't Need a Computer

Oh, darling, I can't wait until we have adorable children so we can plop them in front of a giant TV, shove a screen in front of their faces while we drive through picturesque countryside, then let them drool on our phones while the two of us have lively dinner conversation," said no one ever.

I guess I was in the last wave of parents who didn't have a gazillion electronic options for keeping my children occupied, and I'm glad about that. I mainly relied on a magical bag of books, Hot Wheels, and Legos to entertain the boys while we traveled or waited somewhere. Crayons were the icing on the cake.

Part of my aversion to entertaining children with technology stems from my background in early childhood education and seeing firsthand the damage it inflicts upon developing brains. The other reason I don't like it is because I have, umm, how do I say this . . . common sense. Sure, there are lots of things I don't know, but those topics would bore you, so let's just move ahead and let me thrill you with my expertise. (I'll be sure to save this for my future daughters-in-law someday. They'll love it.)

But seriously now, doesn't it make sense that if a child doesn't interact and observe humans having real-life conversations, they won't know how to converse? And don't you think if a child watches fast-moving, flashy, blinky, beeping things all the live-long day, they'll be bored and find it difficult to focus on, let's say, a plain-old human teacher? How about a boring book that just sits there? Can you spell d-u-l-l?

Down at Miss Penelope's Preschool Ponderosa, the teachers have seen a definite decline in the ability of students to interact and communicate with each other and follow directions. "I used to be able to tell the children to put away the Play-Doh, wash their hands, and sit on the rug for story time. Now, when I give them more than one task, they wander around the room looking lost and confused," said Miss P. "It's like herding cats zoned out on Nyquil when we try to get them to do anything. We've eliminated most field trips because we're afraid one of them will wander away."

I know this sounds extreme, but when my boys were toddlers, I didn't usually let them watch what is considered to be the most popular childhood TV show ever (it involves a big yellow bird), because I found it to be too fast-paced and flashy. Instead, they only watched things like *Thomas & Friends,* which was set in a slower, story-like format, and even that was only every now and then. Unfortunately, *Mister Rogers' Neighborhood,* which was the best children's show ever and filmed with only one camera to simulate an actual, one-on-one personal conversation, had been cancelled by the time my boys were born. Therefore, my husband and I had to model proper conversational techniques ourselves. Shocking!

"But how will they learn to count or say the alphabet?" cried my judgmental friends.

"Um, I think I can handle that. Trigonometry, maybe not, but I can rock my ABCs."

And by the way, both boys qualified for the gifted program and can (almost always) follow directions, unless it involves hanging up a towel.

Although it may come as a shock to many young parents, I promise you, it's okay to have a child do absolutely nothing. In reality, that's when their little brains take off and they learn to entertain themselves. Given a few moments of solitude, little Buford may just think of a way to turn a cardboard box into a sweet-potato processor, or baby Hazel Lou may figure out how to whistle "Dixie."

"Knowing how to entertain themselves and follow directions are the most important skills a child needs to develop before entering school," said Miss Penelope as she lounged on the deck of the local cantina and understandably ordered another margarita.

How was the Greatest Generation ever able to do higher math or memorize extensive poetry and scientific equations without the aid of a computer? Sure, they missed all the fun (and depravity) of the internet, but I'm pretty sure they could put away the Play-Doh, wash their hands, and sit on the rug for story time without getting lost.

# When My Little Boy Learned to Sew

It gives me a great sense of accomplishment to be able to thread my sewing machine. Seeing as I only use it a few times a year, it's a miracle I remember how to snake the thread along the correct path, around the hook, behind the thingamajig, and finally through the needle.

I can't really sew and only made a B+ on the skirt I made in ninth-grade home economics class. Required to wear our creations to school, I carried my skirt in a paper bag and snuck into the bathroom before class to put it on then changed back out of it as soon as possible. Although I'm no Natalie Chanin, I am a master at sewing straight lines. This means I can make curtains, pillows, and stitch around tablecloths. My grandmother, who sewed all four of her daughters' poufy dresses and many of my clothes, would roll her eyes at my definition of "sewing," but the little bit I know makes me feel more domestic than cooking dumplings from scratch.

I had the sewing machine out one day years ago when my youngest son took an interest. He's the curious sort and wanted to look at all the levers and switches. As soon as I said, "Be careful, it has sharp parts," he was highly motivated to use this new, dangerous piece of heavy equipment. At one time, my husband's father owned an upholstery shop, so we told our son about Pop's giant machines and after a quick tutorial, he was off and sewing.

I figured he would just play around with some basic stitches then be done with it, but about an hour later, he proudly showed me his manly apron that tied around his waist and had loops and pockets for all his tools. Then he made some dog toys and a (thin) pot holder for the kitchen.

Not long after that, on a Saturday around 6:30 A.M., my husband and I heard a little voice say, "Mom, can we use the blue fabric in your sewing closet?"

"Um-hum," I said as I rolled over.

A little while later, another voice said, "Mom? Can we use your sewing machine?"

"Sure . . . *zzzz.*"

I started to dream I was hearing clipping, snipping, and sewing noises, and finally, when I roused to a state of semi-consciousness and realized it wasn't a dream, I bolted straight up in bed and shook my husband. "What are the boys doing?" (This is probably the most frequently asked question between us.) We ran into the family room to see our youngest son spread-eagle on top of a large piece of denim fabric and his brother tracing a chalk outline around him *à la* hit-and-run victim. The plan unfolded that they were sewing a "flying suit" with straps that would bind it to their wrists and ankles . . . so they could soar off the roof.

But the best creation my nine year old made was a tiny pillow enclosed in a custom-stitched paper envelope. Leaning against me and looking up with a dirty face and serious eyes, he whispered, "It's to rest your hands on when they hurt." I had contracted rheumatoid arthritis early in life and my son had grown up observing how difficult it was for me to open or lift things and saw how my hands often ached. The jaggedly sewn khaki pillow had threads hanging loose and batting peaking out one side. On the top, he had stitched an L because he's been raised to understand how much we Southern ladies love our monograms. I thought it was the most beautiful pillow in the world.

Sewing proved to be a passing interest, and once my son felt he'd mastered the machine, he moved on to other things, but I've kept the pillow all these years to remember how nice it was when my little boy learned to sew.

# The Miracle of the Mother

Even though there's no maternal element mentioned, the Bible story about the loaves and fishes has always made me think of mothers.

I've never had a problem believing the small lunch was multiplied to feed thousands, but what's difficult to accept is that out of all the people at the gathering that day, the only one to remember to bring his lunch was a little boy. In defense, I guess the Bible only says the boy "had" the lunch. It didn't say he "remembered" his lunch. That makes more sense because, you see, I've raised two boys, and I can't begin to count the number of times they forgot their lunch, homework, or field trip permission slip. One of them once got into the car after school and told me he had to keep his jacket on all day because he'd forgotten to put a shirt on that morning. What Granny said was true: "If their heads weren't attached to their necks, they'd walk off and forget those too."

But after thinking about the Bible story I first heard in my three-year-old Sunday School class, I think the author may have omitted the key figure. The one who really saved the day wasn't the little boy who shared his lunch. Instead, the real hero (other than the Savior, of course) had to be none other than the boy's mother. Don't you think she was the one who ran after this New Testament kid and hollered, "Hey, Billy-Jim! Come back here right now! You forgot your fish!"

"Fish again?" he whined. "You know I'm so tired of fish!

Everyone else gets to eat lamb and fig kabobs."

"Young man, you know your father works hard on his boat all day catching these fish. You should be ashamed to complain like you do."

So off Billy-Jim went, hanging his head low, kicking a rock, and swinging his little *Ten Commandments* lunch box with Charlton Heston on the side. Later in the day, when the Disciples asked if anyone had anything to eat, they found a few people with Tic Tacs in their pockets but nothing of any substance. But when Billy-Jim heard someone needed food, he was quick to offer his lunch, thinking he'd get something better in trade.

And then, behold. The boy who was tired of fish saw his worst nightmare come true. Billy-Jim couldn't believe his eyes when he saw enough fried fish (nowhere does it say it wasn't fried) to feed thousands and thousands of people. "Holy cow!" he said. "You mean, 'Holy fish!'" said St. Andrew.

Although the story only mentions fish and bread, because I grew up on the Gulf Coast, I always imagined the bread was hushpuppies, and at this fish-fry there was an abundance of cocktail sauce, coleslaw, and baked beans. Maybe even grits for the really nice people. I mean, why go to all the trouble to perform a miracle unless you're going to do it right? And of course we know this is the event that invented dinner on the grounds. Thank you, dear God.

As mothers, we often think our efforts don't amount to anything and that absolutely no one is listening to us, but because we love our children, we persist. We repeat ourselves twenty times a day and nag the crud out of them to get our point through their thick heads. Then, when they finally realize they have something of value, something to offer, something to share, God will take it and turn it into something big.

The loaves and fishes story is an example of how God provides for our needs and how our small gifts can result in great and mighty things. But it's also a story that makes me think of all the moms who are behind the scenes, sewing costumes, crawling under the bed to find the homework, repeating themselves a thousand times, and teaching their children how beautiful it is to appreciate what we have then share it with others. Because behind every great miracle there just may be a mother making another lunch.

# Who's the Boss?

As cousin Rosie Belle from Robertsdale was finalizing her Thanksgiving menu, she received a call from her husband's third cousin in Prattville, who informed her that little Brooklyn-Savannah wouldn't be eating the turkey or dressing or for that matter any pumpkin pie at this year's family get-together.

"Oh no!" exclaimed Rosie Belle. "Does she have allergies?"

"No, she just doesn't like that kind of food and will cry if I make her eat it, so could you make something else for her?"

"I liked to have jumped through that phone and jacked that woman to Jesus," said Rosie Belle. "Kids these days are making all the decisions in the family and no one has the guts to stand up to them. On top of that, if you're going to cave in and let them eat something different from everyone else, at least have the decency to provide it yourself."

I gave my cousin a big "Amen, sister," then got out of her way.

Wanting to keep the peace, since everyone was still testy from the elections, Rosie Belle refrained from unloading her silver tongue and told Brooklyn-Savannah's mother there'd be peanut butter and jelly on hand. The distant cousin bristled at that option but said they'd be there nonetheless.

I have to agree with Rosie Belle. It always baffles me

when families let their children be the boss. Parents need to understand that if they allow their four year old to call the shots, they'll soon awaken to a sixteen-year-old dictator ruling their house.

Sure, everyone needs to exercise some sort of authority in their lives, but children can achieve a feeling of control and gain decision-making experience with age-appropriate options like which shirt to wear or how to comb their hair. As they get older, they can decide which sport to try or which instrument to play.

"But Mom!" whined little Lola Mae, "I want to go to the rock-n-roll church that serves Nutter Butters for communion."

"Of course you do, darling," replied her wise mother. "You'd also love it if I turned into Mary Poppins and gave you a spoonful of sugar every time the clock chimed, but that's not going to happen either."

Over-the-top birthday parties that break the bank, a limousine to parade the fourth-grade graduate around town in honor of his perfect B average, not having to visit Grandma because it's so "boring," and eating nothing but macaroni and cheese for six straight years are all the result of bossy children and weak parents.

I read about a father who was horribly upset because his preteens were texting on their phones like zombies instead of engaging in conversation as he drove them to school. Call me crazy, but how about telling them to put the phones away? The title of "father" comes with some privileges, you know. "Hey everybody, I have a new rule. From now on, you can't use your phone in the mornings until we get to the corner of Authority and Respect."

The timid may ask, "Oh dear, what if they don't comply?" That's easy. Take away their phones. Ta-da! "Oh, but I couldn't do that!" Sure you can. Who pays for the phone?

"But they'll whine and argue and I don't like conflict." Then you shouldn't have had children, because conflict is every child's middle name, and it's how they learn, grow, and develop character. If they get their way all the time, they may grow up and not know how to graciously deal with defeat, and wouldn't that be sad?

It's natural for children to test the limits, and it's the job of parents to say both "no" and "yes" at the appropriate times. There's also a big chance that if Brooklyn-Savannah has no choice other than to eat the Thanksgiving spread, she may discover she actually loves turkey and dressing. If not, I'm sure her mommy will stop by McDonald's on their way home.

# Defend Yourself Like Red Chief

Everyone's in an uproar over exactly who should or should not be allowed to enter public bathrooms. Before we label everyone as crazed lunatics trying to grab the kiddies, we should step back for a moment and realize that from the very day children were invented, mothers have always worried that some type of boogey man will try to harm, snatch, or frighten their precious offspring in all sorts of places, not just public restrooms.

There's really no way to look at a person and tell whether or not they are demented enough to harm a child. I've known both a clean-cut man who was nabbed by the FBI for attempted child molestation and a startling-looking person who is as trustworthy as your granny.

It's precisely because we can't judge a book by its cover that I decided to teach my boys the "Ransom of Red Chief" self-defense plan so they would be on guard with everyone, no matter what their appearance suggested. You remember the O. Henry story where the kidnappers grab the redheaded ten-year-old boy from Alabama and hold him for ransom, only to discover that he is a stinkin' terror who drives them crazy. At the end of the story, the two kidnappers are forced to pay the boy's father to take him back.

As painful as it was to push Southern manners aside, I taught my boys it was okay and essential to scream, hit, bite, scratch, gouge, and kick anyone who dared cross the line of decency. My goal was to make any potential predator rue the day he ever laid eyes on my child. If anyone actually attempted to snatch them and run out of a store, my sweeties were instructed to repeatedly poke the eyes of the kidnapper while screaming, "This isn't my daddy!" because we've all seen crying children being carried out by a man and thought, "Poor Dad, he's got his hands full with that one." But then again . . . was he really the dad?

The other thing I taught my children to scream was a word I wasn't even allowed to say as a little girl, but somehow screaming "Pervert!" shocks the offender and often causes them to turn and run. I instructed my boys it was okay to scream this word at the top of their lungs if anyone ever fit the description of what we very carefully reviewed and deemed to be a true pervert. A nice Southern gentleman in the men's room who smiled and said, "Do you need help reaching the paper towels?" was not classified as a pervert and therefore shouldn't be verbally bombed. However, if a man tried to view, touch, or discuss anything normally covered by a swimsuit, he would be a candidate for the full-blown Red Chief treatment.

By the time the boys reached the age where they were too old to go to the ladies' room with me and wanted to enter the men's room alone, they were well equipped to handle any trouble they encountered. But just in case, I pushed my own good manners aside and stood directly outside the door with arms crossed, memorizing the faces and glaring at any man who came in or out while my precious babies were in there. The issue of whether or not the boys washed their hands was suddenly my secondary concern.

Child predators have notoriously targeted children who are meek or can be easily intimidated. By training your child to be bold, spirited, and outspoken, they have a better chance of standing up to evil. Role playing and discussing what they would do in a bad situation empowered my boys, and I suspect there was a superhero part deep down inside them that secretly hoped someone would try to mess with them so they'd have an excuse to open up a kid-sized can of whoop-butt on some deviant adult.

We're living in a strange, scary world, but equipping a child with the courage and tenacity of little Red Chief is a good first step towards protection. And if you think Red Chief can pack a punch against a predator, you should see his mama.

# Cornbread with a Side of Love

It wasn't the flowers, candy, or twirling me across the kitchen floor that earned my husband a gold star on his romance chart. The thing he did that I found to be dreamy and romantic was when he scared the bejeebers out of our son.

First of all, I want it to be known that I really do have two of the most wonderful, honorable, Godly young men you could find anywhere. They are charming, helpful, sympathetic, witty, and yet . . . at the end of the day, they are still teenage boys. *Sigh.*

Just like every other teenager in the world, they've gone through some rough patches and temporarily lost their minds. I've tried to explain that the decision-making part of a man's brain isn't fully developed until age thirty, and even then, it's questionable. We've tried to guide them through their journey of unusual hairstyles, choices in friends, and reptiles for pets, but there never seems to be an end to their strange behavior or wacky ways of expressing their emotions. And that's exactly where the romance came in.

While sitting at the dinner table and reaching for the cornbread, the eldest, who was then in the golden age of middle school, decided to unload and let me have it in no uncertain terms. I can't even remember what he said, or why he said it, but his hormonal words were vicious, hateful, and all around mean, especially when you consider they were aimed at the woman who brought him into this world and put the cornbread on the table.

I caught my breath at his boldness, but before I could say a word, my dear husband snatched the young boy's chin between his thumb and finger, glared into his wide blue eyes, and with the slowness of syrup in January and the bitterness of acid said, "Don't you ever speak to *my wife* that way again!"

Both boys froze in their seats and one gave a little shudder. The beagle even slunk out from under the table and headed for the hallway.

By using the words "my wife" instead of "your mother," my husband took the issue away from me and instead shifted the insult to him. He could have easily said, "Knock it off" or "Watch your mouth," but his choice of words revealed several things to both boys—even the innocent one who was just as bug-eyed as his naughty brother.

Number one, my husband's statement told the boys that their parents are a team. Don't try to divide us, and if you go after one of us, you'll have to deal with us both. Marriage is a partnership and it's not going to be broken in half by some smart-mouthed teenager. In other words, in our house, Daddy doesn't laugh when you pick on Mama, and Mama's likely to come after you if you mess with her man.

Number two, no matter how much we've taught them that women can stand on their own, we live in a beautiful region where gentlemen defend ladies, and that goes double when the lady happens to be your wife. When our boys are married some day, we hope—no, we know—they will do the same for their wives. And if they have a daughter (please, dear God, just one girl), even better.

And third, by using the phrase "my wife," my sweet man laid out a plan of family loyalty. If Daddy defends "his wife," then someday, he'll defend "his son" too—even if that son has a sassy mouth that's begging for a bar of

Ivory soap. Family sticks together and we don't take kindly to those who gnaw on us, whether they're on the outside looking in or sitting at our dinner table sporting a mouthful of braces we paid for.

Come to think of it, maybe the reason I now have two excellent (and still occasionally mischievous but rarely rude) sons is because they have a daddy who loves and defends their mama, and that is the most romantic thing any woman could ever want.

# Just a Matter of Time

Houses reflect the people within them, so it makes sense that they are in a constant state of growth and change—whether we like it or not.

In our first house, my husband and I crawled around and installed safety plugs in all the electrical outlets. We wired the house for monitors and bought nontoxic furnishings made of all-natural materials, lest one of our perfect babies decide to gnaw on the leg of a chair.

The house changed again when we moved the baby bed to storage, added big-boy beds, and stopped locking down the toilet seats. We raised the temperature of the hot water heater, no longer afraid of anyone scalding themselves, and removed the baby gates from treacherous stairs.

The next phase of household adaptability is now in play, but this time it has nothing to do with the children. I'm traumatized that we've had to replace the small, tasteful clock in the bedroom with a large-screened device with giant, glaring numerals. It's a sad sign of redecorating yet to come.

The old clock had dainty, soft luminescent numbers we never really paid attention to because the only time we ever actually looked at it was when we wanted to know if it was time for *The Tonight Show*. We slept like rocks until the next morning and didn't think about the clock at all.

But eventually, the old timepiece started giving us trouble. One night, we were wondering if our son had returned home from an out-of-town football game and my husband groggily asked, "What time is it?"

I opened one eye, then the other, tried to focus, and said, "It's 11:00, no wait, 8:00, no, it can't be 8:00. I think it's 3:37."

"Do you know what time I think it is?" he asked. "I think it's time you get glasses."

Of all the nerve. "I'm just sleepy," I told the rude man in my bed who, please note, was asking me to read the time for him.

But he was right. The smudged clock numbers suddenly looked like evil little red eyes glaring at me in the dark. The more I tried to decipher the jumbled glow, the more it jolted me into a wide-awake state. And to add insult to injury, as if losing my eyesight wasn't bad enough, I suddenly started waking up more often in the middle of the night. Since I couldn't see the clock, I had no idea if I should try to go back to sleep or go ahead and start breakfast. It was like living on the Space Station and having no concept of time.

I finally broke down and bought a new clock that claimed it was "visible for those with poor eyesight," which may as well have said "for those nearing death." The numerals were not only as large as my hand, but also had a glaring blue light so bright I feared an F-18 was going to land in the room. Even though my husband doubted my sensitive and delicate thin eyelid condition, he kindly covered the face of the $10.99 clock with $5.00 worth of tinted plastic film so it wouldn't keep his aging princess awake. The numerals are still large enough for me to see without sending bright warnings to approaching ships. Now in the mornings, our new game is to give each other an accurate play-by-play of our evening activities.

"I had to get up at 1:14, then the dog was snoring and woke me again at 4:30."

"Well, did you hear that car outside at 3:00 A.M.? I

couldn't get back to sleep until around 4:10."

The new clock is just the first hint of what is sure to be a slippery slope into the next phase of changes around the house. The next thing you know, we'll be installing hand rails above the bathtub, removing all the throw rugs, and clapping the lights on and off.

But at least I'll be able to tell you exactly what time the lights go out, because it's all just a matter of time.

# Better Than a Chick Flick

With my college son working at a camp in Mississippi during the summer, I'm home all day with my dear husband, who works in his home office, and son #2, who works on being a teenager. Both of them, right under my feet, all day. *Allll day.*

Not that I don't love every second of being surrounded by their male company. My darling family is a joy, but let's face it, everyone needs a break sometimes. So when my husband announced he had to go out of town for a weekend conference and asked if our son would like to go, I answered for him and said, "Yes! Yes! Yes! He would love it so much. I'll pack his bags now!"

As they pulled out of the driveway, I did the happy mom dance, lined up my chick-flick, boo-hoo movies, pulled out the box of nail polish, glitter, and unicorn stickers we girls love to play with, and readied myself for a few days of relaxing, girly me time.

And then . . . someone knocked on the door.

It was my big, giant, handsome, middle-of-the-woods-smelling son! He drove all the way from Mississippi to surprise me. Oh, joy! Hallelujah! I missed him so very, very much but . . .

"What have I told you about surprising us? You can't just get in your car and drive hours on end without me knowing where you are. And besides, you never know if I'm going to be decent or not. Calling ahead has its benefits, you know."

"Mom, it's 9:00 in the morning and you already have on a dress and heels."

"Well, I almost twisted my ankle trying to put my shoes on when I heard you knock. It was a really stressful moment for me. Two minutes earlier and you would have caught me without pearls. You have to be careful about these surprises."

The truth is, if he'd arrived much later, I would have had a green cucumber mask on my face, mineral enhancing gel in my hair, and a drink with a little umbrella in my hand. This is the stuff that leads a young man to counseling.

The dogs ran in circles around his legs as I adjusted to the idea of rearranging my girly-girl plans.

He could only stay for two and a half days and would therefore completely miss his dad and little brother. There was no food in the house suitable for a giant, hungry college guy because I had planned to eat nothing but chocolate-covered berries and tiny pimento cheese sandwiches cut into triangles, so we made a run to Piggly Wiggly and spent a hefty chunk on buying manly meat, potatoes, sausages, pizzas, and Lucky Charms. We also bought the first full-sized gallon of whole milk we've had in the house since he was home for Christmas.

Cars full of his friends began to arrive, and I began to cook. The TV was never tuned to romantic scenes set in ancient castles. Instead, only science fiction, sports, and loud explosions blared from the screen as college kids laughed and screamed in sheer happiness.

In between visiting with his friends and taking long naps, my son and I ran errands together and actually sat and talked. He's growing up so fast and turning into a young man I'm absolutely crazy about. A few days later, when he pulled out of the driveway to return to Mississippi, I was thrilled to have had him home and couldn't remember the last time I had him all to myself.

Moments after I had finished cleaning the kitchen and

putting away the laundry, my husband and youngest son rolled in from their business trip. They asked, "How was your weekend? Did you get to relax?"

"I'm exhausted but wouldn't have traded one moment of it for all the chocolate-covered berries and chick flicks in the world."

# The Sixteen-Year-Old Trainer

As a teenager, I had the burdensome task of helping my clueless parents understand everything from how to dress to what they should be eating. In college, I took a nutrition class and came home and cleared out their refrigerator of any hydrogenated oils, nitrate-laced meats, and fake dairy creamers. I helped my mother with her hairstyle and felt it was only my duty to show my dad how to choose his shirts. But now, for some reason, my son doesn't realize how smart I am, and he thinks he should be the one telling me what to eat, how to dress, and now, of all things, how to exercise.

One day in the car he asked, "Mom, do you even like to exercise?"

"Oh sure, I love extra fries," I replied, heading to the drive-thru window.

"No, Mom, you really need to start exercising."

"Are you kidding? I exercise all the time. I rarely sit down during the day," I told him as I gobbled down the hot, salty, golden, fried treat.

The sixteen-year-old know-it-all claimed to have researched and found that a woman "my age" (how dare he) should be walking and moving around a lot more than he thought I was. He held me down and strapped an ugly plastic band to my arm and told me I had to wear it so he could monitor how far I walk every day. This Fitbit was synchronized with my iPhone and was going to send me messages to make sure I didn't sit around all day eating boiled peanuts and drinking champagne, as I'm prone to do.

After wearing the ugly bracelet for one day (I tried to hide it beneath rows of pearls), it revealed I had walked 3,000 steps, which I thought was incredible since I didn't leave the house all day except to walk outside to pick a few tomatoes. "See?" I told him, "I'm a blur of constant motion. I'd win the gold medal in the Housewife Olympics."

Teen boy looked at me and shook his head. Through his eyes, he told me I was pitiful.

Incensed by his lack of awe at my physical accomplishment, I did some research of my own and discovered the Fitbit doesn't count your steps unless you swing your arm. Okay, now we know the Fitbit wasn't created by a mother and here's why: Mothers never get to swing their arms. We walk into the kitchen carrying an armload of cups and plates found strewn around the house then see the car keys our husband was searching for, so we take them, along with a stack of mail, his sunglasses, and his phone, and walk them over to his desk. On his desk, we see a dog toy and our child's socks. How they ended up there, we'll never know. So we gather those things up and walk around the house placing items where they belong. Our arms are constantly full and can't jauntily swing back and forth when we are holding a laundry basket, groceries, or the tool box. Our feet are in constant motion, but our hands are occupied.

The one place I'm sure to get a good workout is the grocery store, but, alas, pushing a buggy keeps my arms immobilized while the rest of me is zipping around the bananas. I tried strapping the Fitbit to my ankle, but I looked like Martha Stewart on house arrest and didn't want to start rumors.

By brushing my teeth six times a day, vigorously grating cheese, and occasionally strapping the device to the bouncy beagle's collar and whispering "squirrel," I've upped my count to around 7,000 steps a day, which pleases my son, but only up to a point. He claims I should be walking 10,000 steps a day. Who does he think I am, Jackie Joyner-Kersee?

Exercise is only the beginning. I've got to make sure this kid of mine never takes a nutrition class or there go my French fries, peanuts, and champagne. And for some reason, his meddling in my affairs amuses my parents to no end.

# How to Care for Your Belle When She Isn't Well

As soon as I uttered the sentence, "I haven't had the flu in fifteen years," I felt like a truck of gray mules had hit me hard. I took to bed and blamed the people on my airplane the previous week, who felt it culturally and socially acceptable to cough and sneeze openly into my face. And they say Americans are rude! The crazy Southern weather back home didn't help, with temperatures fluctuating a good thirty degrees or so within the span of a few days.

As I lay sprawled across the davenport, vacant of vigor and fragile of fortitude, I pulled out the list I keep handy for someone I know who sometimes needs a little reminder of the proper way to care for a sick Southern belle.

My husband isn't from around these parts, and as he's learned, Southern ladies require a little more care than the average American female, but he also knows it's well worth the effort. So, in addition to the obvious requirement of making homemade chicken soup and using Great-Great-Great-Granny's silver soup spoons (that still have scratches from being buried in the backyard to keep them hidden from the pesky Yankees), here are a few other pointers I can share in hopes that all true belles receive proper treatment when they're ill.

1. Immediately set the Sunday School prayer chain in motion. Nothing gets done till the Methodists start to pray.

2. Great-Aunt Mae-Rae's crystal decanter with matching drinking glass must be filled and placed next to the bed, which makes the water taste much better than when it comes from a plastic bottle. Crushed ice, not cubed, is a plus.

3. A little brass bell must also be placed next to the bed to alert the help of any sudden needs, such as a pillow fluff or salty crackers.

4. The belle's monogrammed pajamas must match the bedclothes, which must match the extra throw pillows, which all must complement her eye color, no matter how puffy and watery they may be.

5. Pearls? Why, of course! They soothe a sore throat.

6. No paper tissues allowed. Only soft vintage hankies will do, and if they have a hand-embroidered flower motif, they soothe all the more.

7. The caregiver must also remember to cancel all the belle's appointments involving business deals, book clubs, and beauty shops. Even though the contact numbers nowadays are stored in her phone, they can also be found in the tiny little Crane address book located in the top drawer of her organized desk.

8. Reruns of *Downton Abbey, Desperate Housewives,* and *Designing Women* must be queued up on Hulu. Don't worry, she has *Steel Magnolias* memorized and just watched it last week anyway.

9. The belle's favorite dog gets to sleep at the foot of the bed—but this is normal.

10. Once she can lift her poor little head off the pillow, the pampered patient will need her monogramed stationery to immediately begin writing thank-you notes to all those darling enough to send food, flowers, or cards while she was ailing.

Now, let me evaluate my own recovery. Did I get any of this

required care while I was sick? Well, one out of ten isn't bad for my house. And besides, I love that little dog. Can somebody please give me a "Bless your heart?"

# The Not-So-Caring Care Package

Generally speaking, I'm a good mom. My children have always been well fed, clothed, and somewhat protected from the elements, at least while I was watching. I only lost one of them once, but in the end he was found at an elderly neighbor's house watching cartoons and eating Jell-O, so the police forgave me. But as the boys have grown older, there are new mom-challenges for which I'm not prepared and I suddenly feel like a total loser.

I've been horrified to realize that I'm terrible at the art of sending care packages.

During the last two years my son has been in college and away working at summer camp, and I've only managed to get four, maybe five, boxes of goodies shipped to him. And getting those packages delivered was more complicated, and on some level more painful, than delivering the actual child nineteen years earlier!

At the university's recent family weekend, a student spoke to the Parents' Association and gushed about how much it meant when he received the "you've got a package" email from the school's mailroom. With a dreamy look on his face, he told of how he would rush from his dorm down to the student union and tear open the decorated box his mother had packed with all his favorite homemade things, including a needlepoint bookmark she had whipped up with his favorite Bible verse on it. Ummmm . . . Let me think. Last year I sent my son a Darth Vader Pez dispenser and some glow-in-the-dark bracelets.

The problem is twofold: First, I don't know what to include in the package. Second, I procrastinate like heck actually getting it in the mail. I'll put an empty box on the corner of my desk and place a new shirt in it, then I'll stare at the box for a few more days contemplating the contents like a valuable time capsule. I (shockingly) can't include homemade cookies or candy because he's finally decided to listen to what I've been telling him all his life and slow down on his consumption of sweets. He's suddenly Mr. Healthy and only wants nut and berry types of things, so I'll poke around the Piggly Wiggly until I find some dried-fruit-and-sawdust health bars and add those to the box.

I'll spend a few more days thinking about it and eventually toss in some pens and a can of Play-Doh (he liked it when he was five and hasn't notified me of any change), a box of rubber bands for shooting at his roommate, and a new toothbrush, because everyone can always use a new toothbrush.

When I was in college, my mother mailed my chocolate Easter bunny, which arrived completely melted flat with its little pink candy eyes slid cross-eyed over to one side. I scraped it out with a plastic spoon and although it was religiously disturbing, that rabbit was still pretty tasty. She also sent family photos, but nowadays we send our son pictures by text or email. As a young co-ed, I also liked finding an envelope of what my granddaddy called "walking around money," but now we can more safely transfer funds via computer as well, therefore eliminating the need for that bit of excitement.

Looking up his address, finding the big tape gun, remembering to put the package in the car, standing in line at the post office . . . Why can't I be one of the sweet moms with a good attitude about care packages?

Maybe if I remind him of all the times in years past that

I made him homemade, themed birthday cakes, blanket forts, and plaster of Paris volcanoes he'll forgive me for the lame mother-of-big-boys I've become and accept my measly care packages with a grain of salt.

Salt! That's another thing I can include in case he needs to use the family remedy for a sore throat and gargle with warm, salty water. I'll add that to the list for next time. It really is the thought that counts, right?

# Decorating for Boys Is Worthless

I guess it's the kindergarten-teacher gene still inside me that makes me love decorating for holidays—and not just for Christmas or Easter. I really do have boxes of St. Patrick's Day decorations as well as a box labeled "Groundhog Day" that is full of fluffy little rodents in top hats. Every year, I've pulled out the correct storage bin—or bins, for the larger celebrations like Mardi Gras or President's Day—and lovingly adorned our house, thinking in the back of my head, "My boys will always remember our happy house and how we loved celebrating the fun times."

Well, I should have known better.

My son was in tenth grade and asked me where something was. I told him, "It's on the sideboard, next to the Easter tree."

To create my spectacular tree, I had carefully selected long twigs from the yard based upon their shape and fluffy moss content and had arranged them in a large vase and hung happy little Easter eggs, jelly beans, and bunnies from the tips. Remembering the Southern rule "A fluffy bow is the way to go," I tied pastel bows to some of the twigs. Beneath the entire masterpiece, I arranged framed photos of the boys' past Easters.

"What Easter tree?" was his reply.

"The tree on the sideboard in the dining room."

"Oh. When did you put that up?"

"About two weeks ago. We've had dinner in there every night since then. You didn't notice?"

"No."

I was crushed. How would he ever grow up to tell his wife what an awesome mother I'd been if he didn't ever notice how awesome I was in the first place? My awesomeness was invisible, which really depresses an awesome mom. All my hard work was for naught. My festivities and spectacular holiday displays were useless. Meaningless. Senseless.

A few days later, he came swinging into the house and announced, "Hey Mom! I have some friends with me." I heard a commotion and some high-pitched giggles mixed in with the familiar sounds of boys. Girls! Girls were in my house, and I hadn't even checked the bathroom for cleanliness that day! I knew this day would come, and I wasn't ready. Had he warned me ahead of time, not only would I have cleaned, but I would have also made tiny triangle sandwiches. Girls love those. I would have made lemonade from scratch and floated a few lemon slices in the pitcher so they'd be sure and know it was homemade, and I would have definitely put the dog's cute collar on her.

But there was no need for worry. Before I could really get out a proper greeting, I heard squeals and someone say, "Oh, look at the adorable Easter tree!" From there, the girls oohed and aahed over every tiny decoration, photo, and carefully arranged candy in the dish. "Look! All the candy matches the bowl!" said one clever young lady as she gleefully clapped her hands. I wanted to faint from happiness. The other one said, "I love the jelly beans on the tips of the branches. They look like little lights!" I could hardly speak because I thought I would cry from joy. I couldn't believe such incredibly gracious, conscientious, and superbly well-bred humans existed.

The boys called them to come look at the dog licking herself, but the refined females really and truly said, "Hold on, we're still looking at the tree." Death could have knocked on the door at that moment, and I would have gone with him a happy woman.

That night I looked at my sons at the dinner table, who were slurping up their food, and realized it wasn't their job to notice my pretty seasonal décor. Instead their mission in life was to seek out and bring home girls (for me) who will love and appreciate all my pretty things. If only someday I can have daughters-in-law who want to argue over which one will inherit my Pilgrim finger puppets, my work on earth will not have been in vain, and I'll know my boys are in good, creative hands.

# Thy Will Be Done

For the past twenty years, I've prayed for one young lady in particular. Seventeen years ago, I started praying for another. I know hardly anything about them, yet they've stayed on my prayer list month after month, year after year. The only thing I do know about these two young ladies is that someday they will marry my two sons.

I pray: Dear God, I know you are in total control of bringing the perfect young ladies into my sons' lives and you know best who is right for them. I don't even know what these fine young ladies are named, but please let it be something respectable and traditionally spelled so it doesn't look ridiculous on the invitations. I don't know where in the world they live, but Father in Heaven, you know I will break out in a hissy fit topped by hives if they weren't raised in the South.

And Lord, I ask that you give these girls good parents who have taught them right from wrong, parents who have taken them to Vacation Bible School, summer camps, and their grandparents' houses. Let the future additions to my family have mamas that proved their love for their daughters by clipping giant bows in their blonde, red, or light brown hair, because of course those colors will be a good match for my boys' complexions and will look fabulous on future Christmas cards.

You told us, Lord, that beauty is fleeting and the true character of a woman is far above rubies, but would it hurt to let these girls be just a little bit pretty, at least in

137

the eyes of my boys? Actually, would it hurt if my friends thought they were pretty too?

Like your devoted servant Winston Churchill said, "The most beautiful voice in the world is that of an educated Southern woman," so I ask you to please let these future daughters-in-law have the gift of a good education. But I beg you not to send them to the University of Florida because we just can't have that kind of ruckus in the family. You know I'm not asking for these girls to be brain surgeons as long as they can give me brilliant grandchildren. Thank you, kind Creator.

And Father, although I don't demand these precious girls come from entitlement, because that often creates spoiled girls, please let them at least have had the opportunity to attend cotillion so they will know which fork to use. You know how I've threatened my boys over the years by telling them a girl will someday break up with them for using the salad fork for the pot roast. Not that I'm trying to tell you what to do or anything like that, God, but just this once, can you let the boys be amazed that I knew what I was talking about and (the right kind of) girls really do care about such things?

And Heavenly Creator, I trust you will use your perfect timing to allow my boys to meet these girls at exactly the right point in their lives—not too early, because you know how people around here will talk, but don't wait too long either because I still want to look cute in the photos and be able to dance at the weddings.

Gracious God, I humbly ask that you let these two sweet girls fall in love with my home in Alabama and want to live near me and not drag my boys off to the far ends of the earth. But please don't let them think I'll babysit all the time.

But Lord, if for some reason these future daughters-in-love are sad little orphans with no one to teach them about how we should always trust you with every detail of our lives and not try to tell you what to do . . . Well then thank you, God, because I'll get to plan the weddings myself! Bless their sweet little hearts and a big "Amen" to you!

# Operation Lawrence Welk

When we're home on a Saturday evening, and everyone is scattered around the house doing their own thing, I like to slip over, grab the remote control, turn the TV to the PBS station, and crank up *The Lawrence Welk Show.* You should see the teenagers come running out of their rooms, faces filled with horror and clamping their hands over their ears.

With the clicker cleverly hidden under the sleeping dog, no one is able to change the channel, so they are doomed to watch plaid-coated, bouffant-coiffed, ruffled tuxedo-clad performers warble and dance their way across the screen. The eye rolling begins within seconds and the intense whining and griping ensues. "Mom! This is horrible! Why do you make us watch this? Why are they dressed like that? How long will it be before we can watch a movie?" Oh, the sheer agony of hearing old standards like "Singing in the Rain" while fake raindrops fall on girls in plastic polka-dot raincoats is too much for their young minds to handle.

When I would visit my grandparents, we would sit together in the living room and either shell peas or play a card game while Lawrence Welk was on the television in the background. The popular show, which aired from 1951-1982, features wholesome, all-American classics that everyone should know. Even though the musical program has aired in continuous reruns since its cancellation, it has never been a favorite of the teen scene from any generation.

When a young man wearing a mint green leisure suit

swings a suitcase by his side and croons "I'm Leaving on a Jet Plane," the conversation gets pointed. "Why doesn't his suitcase have wheels? What instrument is that in the background? How does he get his hair to do that?"

School curriculum teaches our children classic American stories, poems, and artwork, but not many schools provide an education in the rich history of American music. My wise and wonderful fifth grade teacher understood this need and helped us assemble songbooks we would use every Friday afternoon to belt out the likes of "Oh! Susanna," "Red River Valley," and "Camptown Races." Other than kickball, it was our favorite part of the week.

Once, on the playground, when two boys were racing to the oak tree, someone called out, "I bet my money on the bobtail nag," and we all joined in by shouting, "Somebody bet on the bay!" We doubled over laughing at what clever ten year olds we were for being able to quote Stephen Foster. (It also helped us understand what Foghorn Leghorn was singing in the barnyard on Saturday mornings . . . "Doo-dah, doo-dah.")

Back in front of the TV, as the minutes tick by and chiffon-draped dancers swirl across the stage, miraculously no one leaves the room. Instead, my boys' faux irritation turns to laughter, which evolves into more good-natured snippy comments, and then ends at the desired destination of good, old-fashioned, non-computerized conversation.

"I need to practice my guitar more," says one boy.

"I'll help you put on the new strings," says the other.

They run to get their instruments then return and get to work without even realizing they are humming along to "Goodnight, Irene."

My sinister plan of Operation Lawrence Welk has worked its magic once again. Everyone is together in one room, talking, cracking jokes, and having a nice evening, and at the end of the show, when the cast gathers to sing the signature farewell song that ends with *"Adios, au revoir, auf wiedersehn . . . good night!"* one of the boys always says, "Hey, didn't you sing that to us when we were little?"

Who, me? Where would I have learned such a thing?

Wait a minute, you don't think my grandparents had their own sinister plan to indoctrinate me with those fuddy-duddy songs, do you?

# Senioritis

Several emails a week have been popping up on my computer with titles like "Senior Plans," "Senior News," or "Senior Moments." I was highly insulted at first and immediately deleted them, until I realized that the messages weren't aimed at me but were instead legitimate reminders from the high school guidance counselor and various colleges that my eldest son is now a high school senior.

My son is handling his impending graduation with calmness and maturity. I, on the other hand, am losing my mind. A friend once told me that when your child leaves for college, God somehow makes you ready for them to leave. Really-and-truly ready, as in "Don't let the door hit you on your way out." Teenagers have an uncanny way of pushing us to our limits.

But that time of shoving him out the door has yet to arrive. I know other people may think this same thing about their child, but my son really is different, and I just need a little more time with him. I like having him around.

He's kind, funny, charming, and an all-around great son. He's trustworthy, he makes wise choices, and we've never had to punish him for being (too) late or getting (too) wild. Towels on the floor and not studying enough are the worst we get from him. Of course, as soon as I write this, Murphy's Law dictates I'll be getting a call from the principal or police chief any second, but as for this very moment, I have a really good kid.

My main symptoms of Senioritis usually flare up around three or four in the morning. I'm jarred awake in a total panic, thinking things like "He eats too many sweets. He's going to become diabetic!" or "There's no way he can possibly drive in a big city!" And then there's a string of reminders for myself like "I need to have a spare key made for his car, but then he'll probably misplace it. I need to fix a first-aid kit for him. Better yet, I need to make sure there's a nurse on campus."

The next morning, full of self-induced fear, I try to remain calm and casual as I grab his giant shoulders and yell, "YOU NEED TO EAT MORE GREEN THINGS!" The tall, serene teen then looks down and sighs, "Mom! You've got to stop this."

But how can I stop? He doesn't know everything he should know and I only have a few months left to teach him.

When he was five years old, he swore he would never drive, would attend a local college, and live next door to me forever. I should have made him sign something to make it legal, because now he claims to not even remember any of those sacred promises. On top of everything else, now I have to worry about him having memory lapses.

But for now, he's cool and relaxed, and I'm a crazy fool who keeps looking at his baby photos and digging through the drawer where I saved all his drawings of dinosaurs and R2-D2 he made in kindergarten.

It's perfectly obvious to me why the term "senior" is applicable to both high school seniors and frazzled senior parents. Both groups are on the edge, ready to step into— or be pushed into—unchartered territory. Ready or not, we'll all have to find our way.

Maybe his dorm will need a nice senior housemother.

# III.

## Our Darling Southern Manners

Southerners are known for their manners. As you'll read, there really is a reason we want to teach and practice civility. Holding doors for ladies isn't sexist, it's just kind and a way to honor them. Actually, these days, ladies will hold doors for men if their arms are full or they are in need of help. We're friendly and helpful. There's a fine line between habit and tradition, but the rule is, if it puts others at ease and makes things nicer and easier, then, by all means, do it. We think it's an honor to use our best china and silver to serve you dinner, and if you fuss in protest, you're basically telling us we shouldn't value you and we don't know what in the tarnation we're doing. Bless your heart, and good luck being invited back.

# Southern Manners Serve a Purpose

Yes, ma'am, there actually are rational, common-sense reasons we teach our children manners here in the South. It has nothing to do with tradition and everything to do with making society a more civilized place. And before you think I equate "civilized" with "moonlight and magnolias," hold your horses—please and thank you.

You see, the truth is, we think it's wise to teach our children there's a pecking order in society to which they must adhere. As much as we would like to think we're all created equal—and yes, in God's eyes we are—the real-life truth is whether you like it or not, at some point in time, there's going to be someone who is in charge of you. It doesn't matter if you like your boss, commanding officer, or girlfriend's daddy, to keep the peace or your job, you'll need to show them due respect.

A few years ago, I was driving my sons to school when a police officer pulled me over. Totally frustrated, I stopped and rolled down the window. I knew I hadn't been speeding, and of course we were on a tight schedule, but I placed my hands on the steering wheel in clear sight of the officer and gave him a friendly "Good morning." The officer explained that my tag had expired, but I knew for a fact we had received the new stickers in the mail a couple of weeks before, so even though I didn't agree, I apologized and promised to check into the matter. Sure enough, as we pulled away, now late for school, my youngest son piped up from the backseat and said, "Mom . . . Dad gave me the stickers to put on the car, but I thought they both went on his car."

My sons' lesson that morning was not only how the tag renewal system works, but how even when I felt totally irritated by the entire process (and thought for certain the officer must be blind), I still used good manners and interacted in a respectful and polite way. Though the policeman was younger than me, his title and position in the community were to be respected, and I said, "Yes, sir," "No, sir," and "Thank you" when responding to the man who was just doing his job.

I often wonder what people who verbally or physically assault others were like as children. Were they allowed to openly disrespect their parents and teachers? Did they feel entitled or somehow "above" everyone else? What takes them beyond a civilized and legitimate questioning of authority to the point of attack?

Having been taught to use good manners from a young age, my son can be steaming mad at me for whatever reason it is teenagers get mad, but the next second, he will allow me to walk ahead of him in the restaurant and hold my chair while I'm seated. Angry or not, he knows I'm still his mom, and for that reason alone, I deserve his respect. The ability to control elevated emotions is a skill that needs to be taught and practiced. From simple manners, a civil society is born.

Saying "please," looking someone in the eyes when you shake their hand, and writing a thank-you note to Grandmother are ways of training our children to see others as being valuable and worthy of respect. My husband and sons don't hold the door open for me in a sexist ploy because they think I'm weak, they do it because I'm cherished.

It may seem simplistic to think teaching children to say "Yes, ma'am" will guarantee they'll grow into well-adjusted, respectful citizens, but a solid foundation to anything good always begins with the best materials available. So whether manners are taught in the old-fashioned Southern tradition or in another method from elsewhere, it seems being well mannered just may serve a larger purpose after all.

# The White Shoe Rule

Easter is late this year, but I beg you to please hold off on those white shoes just a while longer. Several self-proclaimed fashion experts have declared it's now okay to wear white shoes any time of the year, but those are the same people who design inappropriate Halloween costumes for little girls. Here in the South, we were taught that bright white shoes shouldn't see the light of day until the ham has been baked, the eggs have been deviled, and the bunny's chocolaty ears nibbled.

Give me a brief moment of your time, and I think I can explain exactly why we Southerners love to—no, *have to*—adhere to the white shoe rule.

The Bible itself says, "To everything there is a season," and I'm pretty sure "everything" includes fashion. Our seasons below the Mason-Dixon Line are so screwy, we can't depend on the thermometer to keep us straight. It's hot one day, warm another, boiling the next, and stifling the remainder of the week . . . and that's just autumn. If you toss in a daily bucket of humidity, even Coco Chanel herself would be tempted to think, "It's so warm, I can wear summery white things year round." (She wouldn't.) But it's precisely because of our warm temperatures that we feel obligated to follow a dress code of sorts so we remember which season we are currently observing.

For those of you ready for the advanced Southern culture class, it isn't just white shoes that get the time-restricted label. Seersucker, sandals, and jaunty straw hats are only seen on die-hard Southerners between Easter and Labor Day as well.

Dallis Mae once broke up with a boy because even though the weather was still on the warm side, he showed up on her doorstep for the fall homecoming dance wearing seersucker. "I was totally shocked," said the wise young lady. "I mean, it says a lot about how a boy was raised to see that sort of thing in October. Why, I wouldn't be surprised if his mama uses dinner forks for cake!"

"Aw shucks," said Wilbur Ray after the breakup, "I only asked her out 'cause her brother paid me ten bucks anyway."

Do you want to debate this issue?

"I have a wild spirit and love to break the rules," you may say.

I'll reply, "Then go ahead and run a red light and see how fun it is to break that rule."

"But running a red light may cause someone to be injured" is your smart comeback.

I say, "Well, your white shoes before Easter are injuring my eyes!"

I learned the white shoes rule like most girls around here. My mother, both grandmothers, great-grandmothers, aunts, great-aunts, seventeen cousins, and forty-seven neighbors told me so. The neighbor on the far corner didn't care, but, then again, she moved into the neighborhood nine years earlier from Pittsburgh and would wear white shoes in the middle of November while standing in her front yard sporting a bathrobe and smoking little brown cigarettes.

Here's the deal: if you aren't a baby, a bride, or a retro nurse with a big blue cape, keep the white shoes tucked away until the sacred fashion day of Easter arrives. This world needs rules. We need order. We need to know what to do. It's like taking a casserole to a bereaved family or dropping peanuts in our Co-Cola. It's simply what we've been trained to do. It's our way of dealing with the harsh, unorganized world.

Outward signs give us inward peace. Seeing the giant red V in Atlanta lets us know we've arrived at the chili-dog nirvana of The Varsity, just as spotting the cavernous mouth of the cement killer shark lets us know we've completed our trek to Gulf Shores. White shoes are the great indicator that life is progressing as planned and another season has opened before us. Spring has officially arrived—whether it feels like it or not.

So after a long, hot summer, when you hear that white shoes are prohibited after Labor Day and you must change your Hanes T-shirts to the fall colors of brown, deep gold, and burgundy, please know it's for the good of Southern society. It brings unity, order, and focus to an otherwise chaotic place that is teased by the spiteful thermometer.

As my mother always told me when I impatiently longed to wear my new Easter shoes a few weeks early, "Good things come to those who white."

# Hats Off at the Table

Bless her heart, my longtime friend Fancy Faye is out there in the dating world again. The stunning beauty is smart and successful but totally without luck when it comes to love. She's rather picky, which can be a good thing, I guess, but she recently dumped a perfectly fine man because he sat down in a restaurant and didn't remove his baseball cap.

"I'd already decided it was peculiar of him to wear his cap when he picked me up for our date since the sun was setting in about ten minutes, but to keep it on while we were eating was unthinkable."

I tend to agree with Fancy. I was raised to believe that men wearing hats indoors, and especially at the table, was the main reason Sodom and Gomorrah was fried, scattered, smothered, and chunked.

I remember the occasion when our extended family gathered around the dinner table and we instinctively bowed our heads and waited for Granddaddy to pray. *Silence.* We opened one eye, then the other, and looked down the table. Granddaddy, who was in his late nineties, stared—no, glared—at first cousin once-removed Keith and finally said, "I'll begin when Keith removes his hat." Keith, who was in his mid-sixties, jumped and fumbled for his cap like a scared little boy and finally flipped it off onto his lap. Feeling the long-forgotten sting of a reprimand from an elder, Keith and the other grown men at the table did their best to stifle their laughter, but the message was definitely received. We don't wear hats at the table.

My own sons pitched a fit when I told them they had to remove their caps inside someone's home (mine), yet the rules stated I could leave my cute little navy straw summer hat with the fluffy white band perched on my dainty head because, well . . . because I'm a lady. (Not that I walk around my own house wearing a hat. That would be silly, and besides, it would totally cover up the tiara.)

In order to prove my point, I enlisted the help of my fourteenth cousin twice-removed, Emily Post, who shocked me with her new, modern view. According to E.P., as we like to call her, men may leave their "fashion" hats (think Don Draper) on in public buildings like post offices, train stations (when was the last time we dashed through a train station?), or hotel lobbies and elevators but must remove them at a long list of locations, including restaurants.

The new twist is that now Emily has a separate set of guidelines for the sportier and more casual baseball cap and, lo and behold, ladies are held to the same rules for caps. The maven of manners says both men and women should remove their baseball caps when being introduced to someone, in a private home, during the playing of the national anthem (I'm really big on that one too), in all public buildings, but, especially, most definitely, absolutely, at the table.

Well, I'll be John Brown! Fancy Faye and I attended a Little League game last spring and she wore the most adorable seersucker monogramed baseball cap and didn't think at all about removing it for the national anthem because of being the fairer sex and all. Besides, her ponytail was pulled through the back opening of the cap and anchored with a bow, so it would have required disassembling her hairdo to get the cap off. Our Southern love of hair accessories and swishy ponytails wasn't taken into consideration by Northern cousin Emily Post, so what are we to do now?

I'll stick to wearing a baseball cap only when I'm working in the yard or throwing out the first pitch at a Braves game. As for Fancy, now that she knows she's broken the rule too, she may just have to give her gentleman friend another chance. My hat's off to her.

# Back in Black

A few months after a cheerful parade celebrating her hundredth birthday, complete with a ride in a convertible Corvette, my great-aunt passed away, and I was thrown into a tizzy trying to find a dress to wear to the funeral. Or should I say a "proper" dress to wear to the funeral?

I searched my closet for my go-to summer black dress but remembered it had become a bit too . . . Let's go with "worn" as opposed to "snug." My long-sleeved wool dress was the only suitable black dress I had, and a July funeral in Jay, Florida, is no place for such an oppressive garment. I own other black frocks, but they are more "night on the town" than "hole in the ground" types of outfits.

Nothing is worse than someone being a little too hoochie-coochie looking at a funeral. I know these days, people accept all sorts of colors when we gather to marry them or bury them, but for a funeral, I just feel a strong pull to the tradition of sad, sorrowful black. I also like it when it rains at a funeral because it's like the whole world is shooting out tears.

People who say they want everyone to wear colorful clothing to their "celebration of life" are getting birthdays and funerals confused. It's the same as if they had a piñata at the service so people would have fun, but then filled it with bees so there wasn't too much fun. "Be happy! Wear red! Then cry your head off 'cause I'm not here anymore!"

The only other set-in-stone color rule in society is for weddings, where the only one wearing white should be the person holding the largest bouquet of flowers and being presented the gift of jewelry. White is for the bride alone, although a few grooms in the 1970s thought they'd give the all-white tuxedo a try. (Not such a good idea after all, was it, Mr. Polka-Dot Underwear?)

Much to my horror, an old girlfriend of my husband's showed up at our wedding wearing white and managed to jump into several photos. I swear on a stack of Bibles I had nothing to do with it, but the poor girl was never seen or heard from again, bless her heart.

My husband's college roommate, John, was raised in the South by a mother from Boston who was extremely proper. After John's date with a promising young lady, we asked him how it went. He gloomily shook his head and said, "I knew she wasn't for me when she answered the door wearing all black before sundown." At twenty years old, I had never heard that rule but was deeply impressed there were still social and fashion rules I didn't know. From that point on, John's mother was my hero, and years later, she attended my wedding and endeared herself to me even more for casting an evil eye at the chick wearing white.

Back to my great-aunt's summertime funeral. I finally settled on a lightweight tan dress with coordinating tan heels, minimal jewelry, and no perfume—because you never want to clash with the flowers. I was suitably subdued, respectfully bland, but still not in proper black.

So if any of you aren't feeling well, I'd appreciate it if you could just hang on a little longer while I find a decent black dress. I promise it will be worth the wait. And if, heaven forbid, it's my turn to be planted in the ground, by all means, wear whatever you'd like. But those in black get preferred seating. And pearls will earn you a souvenir funeral fan.

# Designing (Clowns) Women

I drive to the stores hopeful, enter the dressing room skeptical, and exit the stores frustrated. Welcome to the official decade of ugly ladies' clothing. That may sound a tad bit strong, but, seriously, what are the designers thinking?

Fashion school these days goes like this: first, they recruit color-blind clowns to design the fabric. Pink, red, orange, polka dots, stripes, and floral all get splashed onto one bolt of fabric. Then they have blind, one-armed seamstresses sew up the final product, with exposed seams, unfinished hems, and crooked necklines all being called "stylish."

I'm in a dying clan of women who still like to wear a real dress to church, and store buyers don't even know this category of women exists. Current choices in the stores are either made for the granny who whacks Sylvester the Cat over the head with a broom to free Tweety Bird or for a "saucy-professional" girl. (I'm not talking about a Tabasco company executive.)

After a grueling hunt to find a regular old church dress that didn't look "regular" or "old," I finally found a pretty frock and fell in love with the soft green color, only to spin it around and see a gaudy, oversized gold zipper running down the back. "What are they thinking?" I asked the saleswoman. "Don't they know I can't lean back on the pew with jumbo metal teeth gouging my spine?" The saleswoman shook her head and said, "I know. Everyone complains about them, but after the giant zipper has been around a while, the ladies will warm up to it and start to accept it as stylish."

So that's their plan. The fashion houses are playing a version of "The Emperor's New Clothes." If they can force us to wear something hideous by limiting our choices, we'll eventually say we like it to justify the purchase . . . or maybe we won't. Now I understand why people hang on to their old clothes and wear things from past decades. It's because they can't find anything better.

After you've lived a while, you learn that if you spend a few extra dollars on a well-made, timeless item, you'll save money in the long run. I discovered this lesson when years ago, my mother, who knew I needed a little treat, phoned and said I could use her Gayfer's charge card to buy myself a new dress. Knowing there was nothing better in this world than a new dress from Gayfer's, I dashed over to the large department store after work and found the perfect navy blue, double-breasted, fully lined, sleeveless dress with a full circle skirt. It had a double row of embossed gold buttons down the front and wasn't even part of the Moonlight Madness sale.

That was twenty years ago, and thanks to the invention of multiple holes in the belt, I still fit in the dress—although I haven't worn it in a few years for fear someone from twenty years ago will recognize it. When my husband suggested I replace the frock, I began to hunt for a newer version. And do you know, there's no such thing as a classic, navy blue, double-breasted, fully lined, sleeveless dress with a full circle skirt anymore? The closest thing I've found has been a much cheaper version that didn't look like it would hold up in the rain, let alone for another twenty years. It also had pink piping on the hem and a big gold zipper down the back.

And don't get me started on shoes. I think the designing clowns have been hard at work on those as well.

# Counting Blessings at Cracker Barrel

Years ago, I taught in the prekindergarten program in an inner-city public school and realized the students were confused when we read stories about Santa Claus. I finally grasped that it wasn't the jolly old elf who puzzled them, but the concept of a fireplace was totally foreign to a group of children who lived in government-owned apartments. We had recently learned about fire safety, so a story about someone landing in a "fire place" . . . Well, you can understand their confusion.

I thought about how I could show the children a real fireplace, and it finally dawned on me that the perfect example of Southern hospitality with collard greens, sweet tea, and a roaring fire was a short drive away at Cracker Barrel.

The manager agreed to host our class, and for just a few dollars per student, the restaurant would provide a hot biscuit, scrambled eggs, sausage, and milk, all served in front of their trademark stone fireplace. Since the school cafeteria only used plastic spoons and milk cartons, and the only time these children ate restaurant food was when it was a hamburger or taco from their neighborhood fast-food joint, we launched into lessons on proper table manners in preparation for our visit.

The students were dressed in their fanciest outfits as we pulled the bus up to the rustic-themed restaurant, and their faces showed pure amazement over the bounty of pretty things in the gift shop. Other customers raised their eyebrows as we followed the waitress (which was another thing the children had never seen) to the tables.

The honored pint-sized customers scrambled into their chairs and placed the napkins in their laps, then broke into big smiles when they saw real drinking glasses. Only one thing was lacking. Even though it was the middle of January, the weather outside was a balmy Southern 78 degrees, and therefore no fire was flickering.

Once I reminded the manager of our ultimate purpose, he kindly built a roaring fire, which brought gasps from my wide-eyed students. I think the employees had to crank the air-conditioner down a few notches, which is a typical Southern reaction when we use fireplaces anyway, but they were gracious and kind as they treated the children like royalty.

Later that year, I also took the class on their first visits to the mall, movie theater, and airport. You'd have thought we were visiting the Vatican when they saw the main terminal with all the beautiful artwork and architecture, details most people rushing past don't even notice.

I tried to involve the parents in these trips and help them understand that riding the city bus to visit free museums or to spend a hot afternoon in the cool library for story time was within their reach and could greatly expand their child's world, but many were reluctant to visit unfamiliar places, although most were located less than ten miles away.

Appreciating seemingly small niceties in life like knowing what a fireplace is or using a real knife to butter your biscuit is something most take for granted. I realized that wealth thrown at schools isn't always the answer to producing well-educated children. Instead, it's the wealth of experiences that opens the world to curious minds and encourages a lifetime love of seeking, exploring, and learning new things.

Like most teachers, I was exposed to all types of personal family situations and learned that even in the swankiest of communities full of fabulous cultural opportunities, there are children who sit all day in empty homes with distorted television shows being their only link to the outside world.

Perhaps pre-K programs needn't be an option for all children, because as wonderful as it is, a good home life full of enriching activities is still best for young children and kindergarten comes fast enough. But for those who are living in poverty or other critical conditions, I know in my heart that a simple brunch in front of the fireplace at Cracker Barrel can be a life-changing experience. For both the student and the teacher.

# Tips for a Perfectly Proper Audience

*This next story was loved the most by principals, dance instructors, and piano teachers. I heard both funny and terrifying feedback about the real-life behavior of those who have attended concerts over the years. Gum chewing used to be the biggest sin of audience members, but with the invention of cell phones, cameras, and spandex, some people show up thinking they're the ones putting on the show.*

*All I can think to say is "Mercy daisy, and bless their hearts."*

Well, well, well . . . What have we here? Could it be a springtime graduation or recital? How about an end-of-the-year awards ceremony? It's a good thing the Alabama chapter of the Committee for the Preservation of Loveliness has issued new guidelines, and they're not for the graduates or award winners. Instead, we've just updated and revised the standards of behavior for the most important element of all productions: the audience.

Ahem, now that we have your undivided attention—which in this day and age is a difficult thing to do—let's start with the attendee's appearance. Those who take to the stage are often required to wear nice clothing or a cute costume, so the audience should also wear their best. Please notify Paw-Paw that his overalls and Flora-Bama baseball cap will have to wait until another time. Ditto for cousin Clawdine's tank top that says, "We whooped the *#@& out of LSU."

Trust us, it won't kill you to put on proper slacks and a shirt with a collar or a lovely spring dress, but just in case, emergency personnel is usually present during such events so you'll be well cared for if you have spasms or break out in a rash from actually tucking in your shirt and wearing a belt.

And unless your darlin' Tiphany Rae is graduating from the Hoot-n-Holler School of Fashion Design and Typing, there's no need to wear your stretchy rhinestone tube top. Regular old schools call for regular old non-sparkly clothing.

The next order of business is to know your surroundings. Are you in a concert hall watching little Mae-Mack dance across the stage in the role of lead possum in the production of "All Things Bright and Beautiful?" Well, her stunning performance calls for hearty applause (hand clapping) and perhaps a quick, yet enthusiastic call of "Bravo!" Fist pumping and shouts of "Woo! You go girl!" are reserved for outdoor events such as hog callings.

Are you sitting in a hot football stadium watching graduates teeter across the field in high heels and slippery-soled dress shoes? In that case, I guess we can bend the rules and allow for a brief verbal affirmation of the graduate's name, as in "Way to go, Pickles!" But here's an addendum: you are the only one who thinks your air horn or cow bell is a good idea. So unless you are attending a Mississippi State football game or a cattle show—I know it is sometimes difficult to tell the two apart—please save all noise devices for when you are stranded at sea.

Is your recital in a house of worship? Some don't like to cheer, clap, or shout in their church out of reverence and fear of waking Jesus, while others feel the need to make sure He knows, along with everyone else, that they've shown up, so just take your cue from the regular attendees.

The last issue the committee addressed was that of clods who think they can head for the exits before the ceremony has concluded just because their twins, Jaxsin and Braxsin, have received their "good effort" certificates and they want to beat the traffic. Here it is as nicely as the committee could phrase it: sit the gosh-darn heck down! Apologies for the vulgarity of the language, but to leave before the entire ceremony is complete is the ultimate lack of good breeding. I promise you, the Golden Corral will still have plenty of gravy on the buffet, so there's no need to climb over legs and step on the toes of others before the final curtain call. Who knows, there may be a future Martin Luther King, Jr., Pavarotti, or Baryshnikov on that stage, and wouldn't it be a pity to miss one single second of the inception of what could be a stellar career?

Now, turn off your phones, curtail the talking, and for crying out loud, no one needs that much chewing gum in their mouth. Congratulations to your loved one, and by all means, we hope you enjoy the show.

# Dear Brides, Please Reconsider the Dress (or, Five Wedding Dress Tips)

If you are easily offended, I beg you to stop reading now. My mother will surely call and say, "Quit being ugly," but I just can't help myself. In defense of their beautiful daughters, the Ladies Auxiliary of the First Self-Righteous Church of Baldwin County won't speak to me next Sunday, but I feel it is my mission in life to spread the truth.

If you insist on proceeding, take a deep breath, and don't say I didn't warn you.

Brides, please . . . Reconsider your decision to wear a strapless dress.

Since 2004, every single bride who has walked down the aisle has worn a strapless dress. And I know if you were one of them, I'm sure you were the one in a thousand who looked fabulous. You probably lifted weights for three years straight, were under the age of twenty-five, had a one percent body fat ratio, and didn't go around all night tugging at the top. I'm sure you were the perfectly beautiful, well-fitted, strap-free bride.

Of course you were.

But for all the others who are considering this path to free your upper arms, please consider these five crucial points.

  1. Don't you want to be original? Don't you want to be unique? This is a big day in your life. Do you really

want to follow the crowd and look like every other girl? You are under the assumption that your dress is different because it has a bow in the back and the others have tiny, fabric-covered buttons, but here's a news flash. In photos, they all look the same.

2. Do you want to be the focus of attention, or do you want your bosoms to steal the show? Last year, a bride tried to give me a hug but couldn't raise her arms for fear of revealing her "maids of honor." She looked like a satin-covered Tyrannosaurus rex with little bitty short arms trying to knock back champagne while squeezing her elbows to her ribs. The highlight of the night was watching her try to throw the bouquet. Mercy.

3. Your photo in the *Daily Doodle* society section will just look like you are nekkid as a jaybird. Last week, four brides were featured in the paper and they all appeared to be wearing nothing but a towel. Three wore pearls; one did not (rebel).

4. Many churches will require you to cover your shoulders anyway. Isn't this a big enough hint from You Know Who?

5. The most beautiful brides in the history of the world, Princess Diana and Jacqueline Kennedy, wore dresses with tasteful sleeves, and look how happy their marriages turned out to be. Well . . . Okay, you've got me there.

And remember, you never know what good will come from sporting feminine sleeves. Scarlett O'Hara's wedding dress from her first marriage to the unfortunately doomed Charles Hamilton boasted sleeves big enough to hide the family silver from the Yankees. Now that's a smart bride if I've ever heard of one.

So, once again, my deepest apologies to the Ladies

Auxiliary and their lovely daughters. But someone had to say it.

(Oh, I didn't want to go to your old wedding anyway!)

# Candlelight Supper and Beagles

Not long ago, my family watched the Westminster Kennel Club Dog Show. Out of 2,700 competitors, the triumphant pup was a bouncy beagle who went by the name of Miss P. The "P" stood for "Peyton," but more appropriately for a breed that is hard headed and hard to train, her registered name was Tashtins Lookin for Trouble.

Trouble indeed. As the owner of a pure-bred beagle, I can tell you it is one stubborn dog. Sweet as the day is long, loyal as a royal servant, cute as . . . well, as cute as a beagle puppy. There's nothing in this world cuter, and that's the precise reason we were lured into taking the howling, ill-mannered hound home with us.

My beagle is named after Superman's longtime love, Lois Lane, because when we adopted her nine years ago Superman was all the rage at my house. She was born into a family of show dogs but was thought to have issues with the shape of her tail, so her show days were forgotten and she was sent to live with us. As it turned out, her tail grew to have the perfectly desired flag shape after all, and since she overheard this bit of information, Lois Lane has not let us forget the star she could have been.

We quickly learned the number one rule to owning a beagle is to keep all food out of reach. Beagles will eat until there's nothing left, whether they are truly hungry or not. We accidentally left her in the garage one day with a forty-pound bag of dog food, and, after a few short minutes, we realized where she was and flung the door open to find the bag ripped down the side and Lois's belly the shape of a basketball.

Lois Lane has eaten the candy from Easter baskets, Christmas stockings, and an entire chocolate birthday cake. We called the veterinarian in a panic, but when he remembered Lois was a beagle, he assured us she would be fine—and she was. Beagles' stomachs have a way of digesting forbidden chocolate as well as buttons, rocks, onions, and potatoes they dig straight from the garden.

After a successful and quite elegant (if I say so myself) candlelight dinner party (Hyacinth Bucket would have been proud), I told my guests to please leave everything where it was on the dining room table, and we would move into the living room for coffee and dessert. As I was serving the coffee, I happened to look over the head of one of the guests in time to see Lois Lane casually trotting around on top of the dining room table, licking every dish clean! "Excuse me one moment . . . Honey, do tell the story about the time we saw a haint out THAT WINDOW OVER THERE!" When everyone turned their heads to look for the haint, I made a running slide across the foyer and dived over a chair to grab the four-legged beast who was just finishing off her fifth plate and moving in for the butter dish. I gave a little "cough-cough" to muffle the sounds of Lois squealing like a baby pig and a fork clanking to the floor.

Table dances aside, Lois usually shows great class and cleverness. She likes to be fed at precisely 4:00 every afternoon, and if I'm lyin', I'm dyin'—she knows how to tell time. At five minutes till four, she sits at my feet and stares me down with laser beam eyes. At 4:00 on the dot, she begins to give a high-pitched whine and finally moves into the beagle howl if I don't get up and feed her.

She's trained me very well, and I have to do what she

says or else she's threatened to make a repeat appearance at my next dinner party. Someone needs to remind her she ain't nothin' but a hound dog.

# Hospitality Never Dies

I delivered not one but two 7Up pound cakes this past week to friends who were suffering from one affliction or the other. Now, in and of themselves, 7Up cakes have no proven healing qualities and have never claimed to cure a thing, but we all know that like the salt water of the Gulf, the gift of food from a friend is good for what ails you.

The first cake went to cousin Rosie Belle in Robertsdale, who had a serious hitch in her get-along resulting from an accident involving her treadmill. It seems while she was trotting along, she propped up her iPad and was watching an old YouTube video of Andraé Crouch's funeral service when the Spirit took hold of her and she lifted her hands in praise and/or worship, lost her balance, and nearly slung herself through the wall. She thought she was a goner as she lay there on the floor of the spare bedroom, and just before she passed out, she heard, "Hallelujah, hallelujah, we're going to see the King!"

The next cake went to a friend who, during last week's big storm, was injured in a lightning strike. She wasn't actually struck by lightning, but when it suddenly hit a pine tree right in her own backyard, she jumped and dropped a can of pineapple on her bare foot. "I usually prefer the fresh pineapple" she explained, "but you know what everybody's sayin' about putting the real thing in your shopping cart at Publix these days. I can't risk someone thinking I'm that kind of woman, so I've been buying the canned Dole." Well, the canned fruit nearly took her toe clean off, but at least she's not being "discussed."

Taking food to friends is a soothing form of kindness and love. Years ago when I was both ill with the Virus and down with the Sadness, my friend Shirley showed up at my house with a little tin of homemade cheese straws. First of all, the warmhearted gesture alone was enough to lift my spirits, but having Shirley remember I specifically loved her cheese straws more than any cake, cookie, or pie made it even better. Her sweet efforts and savory snack healed my broken spirits in no time flat.

My sweet friend Shirley, who stretched my name into six slow syllables, passed away a few weeks ago, and now I'll never have her amazingly perfect cheese straws again. But what I do have from Shirley is the example of how to get out and share the gift of hospitality with others. Shirley not only brought me a delicious cheesy snack, but she also delivered an excellent example of what it means to be a thoughtful friend.

As I packed the 7Up cakes in boxes to take to my cousin who was all stove-up and my friend with her foot cut to pieces (but her virtue still intact), I thought of Shirley and how she would be so happy to know that her example of deep hospitality will live on and continue in those who knew her.

And she'd be totally baffled by the pineapple reference—which would make me love her even more.

## 7Up Cake

1½ cups softened butter
3 cups sugar
5 large eggs
2 tbsp. fresh lemon juice
1 tsp. vanilla
3 cups all-purpose flour
¾ cup 7Up

## Glaze

1½ cups confectioners' sugar
1 tbsp. lemon or lime juice
1-2 tbsp. 7Up

Preheat oven to 350 degrees. Grease and flour a 10-inch bundt cake pan or tube cake pan. In a large bowl, cream butter and sugar together. Add eggs one at a time. Beat in lemon juice and vanilla. Add flour a little bit at a time, alternating with 7Up until all the flour and 7Up are incorporated. Pour batter into cake pan and bake for 60-70 minutes, or until a toothpick inserted into the center of the cake can be removed clean. Let cake cool for 20 minutes then remove to a rack.

After the cake has completely cooled, mix glaze ingredients together, adding small amounts of 7Up until the desired consistency is reached. Drizzle glaze over top and enjoy!

# It's Hard to Say Goodbye

We were all standing on the porch, hugging necks, laughing, and saying, "Come here and give me a little more sugar before I go," but my husband was sitting alone in the dark car, his hands tightly gripping the steering wheel, veins ready to burst. I couldn't figure out why he had suddenly become cross. We were just saying goodbye.

This pattern seemed to go on for years, until my friend mentioned how hard it is for Southerners to say goodbye. She told me how her relatives end the long family visits in Louisiana by getting up to leave and forty-five minutes later, they are all still in front of the house, stuck in departing mode.

And that's when the light bulb went off. My husband's idea of saying goodbye was completely different than mine. And it only took me twenty years to figure that out?

Bless my sweet husband's heart, he's not from around these parts, and he wasn't accustomed to the goodbye ritual. I, however, have never known anything different. Although now that I think about it, when we visit his parents, I've always thought saying goodbye to them seemed rather abrupt.

My Northern in-laws have never walked outside to stand in the driveway and wave till their arm hurt like Granny did on the *Beverly Hillbillies* in the closing credits. Remember what the announcer said: "Take your shoes off. Y'all come back now, y'hear?" My in-laws take a more direct approach. Bob announces, "Well, I guess it's time we get going."

Their response? "Okay (*quick hug*), goodbye."

That's it? I don't need to roll the car window down for one more story from Pop? Nope. We can see through the windows that Pop's already back in front of the TV set before we put the car into reverse.

After spending the day with my Southern relatives, we'll finish the supper dishes and say, "Well, I guess it's time we hit the road." That's Granddaddy's cue to retrieve a pocketknife from a drawer to give to my son, accompanied by a story of how he came into possession of the knife. Grandmother will start in with "Let me get you some scuppernong jelly I just made. And how about some fig preserves too? Come in here and help me. The jars are in a box, slid under the bed in the guest room."

Then an aunt will say, "You need to take some of this ham home with you. We can't possibly eat it all," and off she'll go to find the ziplock bags. My mother will be running around looking for scissors so she can cut out a newspaper article about an old boyfriend of mine who just got released from prison (white collar "incident," of course), but it's okay because now he's going into the ministry.

Cousin Big-un will always tell one more joke, and his brother Lil-un will want to discuss football.

An hour later, we finally pull out of the driveway with everyone standing in the yard waving goodbye until our taillights fade to tiny specks. My husband, so overcome with deep emotion from family time, can hardly speak.

It's not just kinfolk who adhere to this ritual. It's most Southerners in general. Last Tuesday, I picked up my friend Donna Jean for a forty-five-minute coffee date. When we returned to her house, we sat in the driveway for another forty-two minutes talking about how nice it was to go get coffee.

Churchyards across the South are filled with friends

laughing and talking after Sunday services, but You Know Who always manages to grab my hand and pull me off to the car. We once went to Waffle House after church and when we were on our way home, there were still people standing beneath the trees in the churchyard saying goodbye.

The revelation that there is more than one way to say goodbye was a complete shock. I've thought for so long that my sweet, cranky Yankee husband was just plumb wore out from all the fun. In reality, I now realize that maybe he just needs a little more sugar. And another twenty years to get used to it all.

# IV.
# Our Delicious Southern Food

You can't visit the South without tasting some of the best food in the world. Contrary to popular belief, we don't fry everything. Sometimes, we just scrape it off the road and grill it. (Ha-ha! Just trying to do my part to keep too many folks from moving here!) To balance the heaviness of our favorite dishes, we also love to eat fresh vegetables, so you'll see lush gardens in many backyards, a legacy of our rural, agricultural heritage.

Southern food has qualities that do more than just fill and nurture. Our food draws us together in friendship and love, whether it's a lunch shared by two elderly love birds who are enjoying freshly picked okra, Silver King corn, sliced tomatoes, and warm cornbread or a family sitting down to barbecue that's been smoking all day in the backyard or perhaps it's friends huddled together under a small tent in the parking lot of the football stadium, nibbling deviled eggs, fried chicken, and pimento cheese sandwiches. Food is yet another way we celebrate the joy of being together with those we love . . . in the place we love.

191

# The Greatest Love of All

It's often said that food equals love, and there's no more powerful proof of God's love and downright favoritism for the South than His ultimate gift of dinner on the grounds. A gift like this deserves gratitude and shouts of celebration, but, sadly, I think our generation has let the ball drop, and the joy once found in the best meal of the year is slowly fading away.

Maybe our mothers were too busy bringing home the bacon in the '70s and '80s to teach us proper Jell-O mold and creamed-soup casserole etiquette, or maybe we've just sat in front of Pinterest so long looking at pictures of pretty food we don't understand how to actually make it come out of our kitchens. Whatever the reason, it's time to turn things around and start a proper dinner on the grounds revival.

Old photos stuck in drawers at Grandmother's house show ladies in pretty dresses with aprons tied 'round their waists, busily piling heaping platters of food on long cement tables. The tables were a permanent feature beneath the live oak trees on the graveyard side of the church, where they stood strong beneath the weight of generations of homemade dishes. Dinner on the grounds was outdoors or, literally, on the church grounds because there was no such thing as large, air-conditioned fellowship halls or giant Christian life centers with two gyms, fifteen large-screen TVs, and enough room for praise bands to repeat themselves till kingdom come. God's green earth was seen as an economical and beautiful setting for a church feast. Everyone pitched in to cook and clean, and music usually accompanied the event to make the day lively.

Women cooked for days ahead of time to make homemade casseroles, breads, and pies. Placing the food on beautiful plates and platters, they'd carry them in a basket and share the feast with their church family. Nowadays, the idea of dinner on the grounds remains appealing, but many don't understand the mechanics of the meal and they'll show up with a family of eight and bring a tiny bowl of canned green beans, not because they can't afford better, but just because they don't know better. Last year, the chairwoman of the Ladies Social Circle had to run down to the Quickie-Mart to get more fried chicken because the food contributions were so skimpy. Worse yet, it seems just about everyone brought store-bought vittles with the price still stuck to the container. I think every cotton-picking cake was store bought. How have we sunk so low?

There was a time when all Southerners worth their weight in grits understood that deviled eggs belonged on a proper deviled egg plate and store-bought chicken was acceptable if it was presented on Granny's Depression glass platter. Everyone put forth great effort to make sure their food was properly displayed, and thanks to a strip of masking tape bearing your name on the bottom of your Pyrex, no one needed to use flimsy aluminum foil trays for their casseroles.

Because modern-day society dictates we aren't worthy unless we're busy and frazzled, the organizers now often think they're being helpful by simplifying things and assigning dishes according to last names. You know, A-E bring salad, F-J bring a main dish, and so on, until Mrs. Ziffelthorpe gets stuck with the paper goods, which is actually what most people want to sign up for now anyway.

The problem with this A-B-C method is if you put Marva Mae in the salad group, everyone will be crushed because she's the only one who knows how to make chicken and dumplings. Ray-Ray likes to contribute his mouthwatering pulled pork that he smokes all night, but odds are he'll be assigned to bring ice. And, of course, Sally Jane, who's never stepped foot in her newly renovated eighty-thousand-dollar kitchen, will have to bring a main dish, which means she'll fling something from Taco Town on the table—still in the cardboard box. You can see why this well-meaning plan never works. The point of the meal is to demonstrate our faith and trust that it will all work out, and just like the first recorded dinner on the grounds, when two fish and five loaves of bread were somehow turned into a down-home, foot-stomping fish-fry, by God's great guidance, our scattered pieces always result in a unified feast.

A well-heeled dinner on the grounds features every variety and type of vegetable currently being grown within a fifty-mile radius. Corn on the cob, corn cakes, creamed corn, corn salad, and corn bread are displayed with great care. Fried and stewed squash are placed alongside beans that are stringed, red, butter, snapped, and baked. Casseroles are steaming hot and have used up every can of creamed soup in the county. Meats are plentiful and often involve recipes that begin with "First, you get your gun."

Children's eyes grow wide and wives give their husbands an elbow to the ribs at the sight of the dessert tables (plural intended). At a dinner done right, there will be enough desserts to open a bakery. Cakes, pies, tarts, cookies, and always a made-from-scratch banana pudding—or two—will be the grand finale.

On the rare occasion that the Baptists, Methodists, and Presbyterians all have their dinner on the grounds on the same day (It's happened twice in my life and everyone thought it meant Jesus himself was coming back. But whose church would he stop at first?), the Piggly Wiggly will place a special rush order on an extra pallet of the sweet Southern trio: granulated, brown, and powdered.

After what seems like the longest prayer of the year, with children inching closer and closer to the table, the line forms and the fun begins. Visiting with everyone as you fill your plate is half the fun, and discussing the food is the highlight of the day.

"Did your Carol Anne make this Jell-O salad? I love the little pineapple bits she puts in."

"Would you look at this strawberry cake? I swanee, it's the prettiest thing I've seen all week!"

Somewhere deep in the Methodist Book of Order, it dictates, "Thou shalt only place a small portion of each item upon your plate." That means no loading up on one particular dish, even though the top is covered in melted marshmallows and you happen to love melted marshmallows. I always had to watch my boys like a hawk to keep them from taking a whole plate of brownies or all the chicken legs. They knew if I caught them breaking the rules, they'd have to wash the casserole dishes when we got home.

The new trend of having quick coffees-cafés-brunches-and-luncheons has gotten us nowhere. Everyone's rushing around with no time to sit and visit. Our failure to teach the lost art of dinner on the grounds will surely come back to haunt us when our own children grow up and want to join churches that have drive-thru communion.

Preparing the feast is as important as sharing the feast. Taking the time to cook for friends and those we love can be one of our most joyful acts of service. Feeding stomachs is akin to feeding hearts. To work, worship, share, and linger in the company of those we love is a blessing, and we discover the effort we put into dinner on the grounds is worth it. No one leaves hungry, no one leaves sad. A happy extended family has broken bread, and the tradition is once again passed on.

Someday, in the sweet by-and-by, when I'm invited to the heavenly feast, I'll take a peek at the bottom of the bowl of fried okra and see a strip of masking tape bearing the name "St. Peter," and then I'll know I'm with people who understand how to show the greatest love of all.

### Country Chicken and Rice

Although it's not a casserole, chicken and rice is always a favorite dish at Southern gatherings. Lighter than chicken and dumplings, chicken and rice still has a savory flavor without being heavy with cream. At our house, when someone says "Chicken and rice," everyone chimes in with "Hey, that's nice!"

1 whole chicken, approximately 4 lb.
3 cups chopped celery
1 large yellow onion, diced
1 tbsp. salt
1 tbsp. pepper
1 tsp. oregano
1 tsp. celery salt
1 tsp. dried parsley
3 cups long-grain white rice
Salt and pepper to taste

Place chicken in a large pot and fill with just enough water to cover the bird. Add celery, onion, and spices then bring to a boil. Reduce heat and simmer for at least an hour. The longer you let the chicken cook, the more tender and flavorful the dish will be.

Remove chicken from the pot and set broth aside in a separate container. Allow chicken to cool, then pull meet from the bone. Measure 6 cups of broth back into stockpot. Add rice and chicken. Bring to a boil, then reduce heat, and simmer for 15 minutes. Add 1 cup of remaining broth. Simmer for 5 minutes or until rice is cooked.

Add salt and pepper to taste.

## Tuna Noodle Casserole

Casseroles with chicken as the main ingredient are plentiful at dinner on the grounds, but there's always one rebel who delights us all with the ever-popular Tuna Noodle Casserole. Such a classic, the Pyrex dish is always empty within minutes. I've seen this favorite topped with crushed potato chips, crackers, and even crunchy Chinese noodles, but cousin Rosie Belle from Robertsdale prefers this breadcrumb topping. Variations abound, yet the one unifying ingredient you'll always find is that ubiquitous can of creamed soup. That's what has made this casserole delicious, quick, and affordable for generations of cooks.

1 10 oz. can cream of mushroom soup
1 cup milk
4 tbsp. butter, divided
1 cup diced onion
1 cup diced celery
2 cups frozen peas
2 12 oz. cans tuna in water, drained
4 cups cooked wide egg noodles (slightly undercooked)
4 tbsp. dry breadcrumbs

In a large bowl, mix soup and milk together; set aside. Use 2 tbsp. of butter to sauté onions and celery until tender. Stir cooked onions and celery into soup mixture; add peas and tuna. Spread cooked noodles into a casserole dish. Fold soup mixture into cooked noodles. Bake for 30 minutes at 350 degrees. Melt remaining butter and stir into breadcrumbs, then sprinkle buttered breadcrumbs over the top of the casserole. Bake 5 more minutes or until golden brown.

# My Shameful Southern Secret

It's something I've had to hide my entire life, but it's time I come clean.

*(Deep breath.)*

I'm a Southerner, and I don't like sweet tea.

I know, I know. I've had to pretend to sip ladylike on the brew for years. There's no getting away from it around here. Whether it's a business meeting, ladies' luncheon, or a gathering of friends on the front porch, you can bet your bottom dollar, there will be tea. Always cold, always sweet, every season of the year, a glass of sugary sweet iced tea is being placed in your hand.

Now, don't let this shortcoming lead you to believe I'm not Southern. Honey, my Alabama-born mother raised me right. I don't wear white shoes before Easter or after Labor Day, I either monogram or fry everything that doesn't breathe, and all these years later, I still dream about my sorority sisters and wake up singing or thinking I'm passing a candle around a circle. I planned my wedding around the college football schedule, and I cook almost every one of my meals in my grandmother's cast-iron skillet. I'm as bonafide Southern as my beagle is pedigreed.

My short defense as to why I don't like tea is that it's just too dang sweet! I feel like I'm drinking liquefied chocolate cake, minus the chocolate. I know for some of you that would be heaven, but I'm more of a salt lover and don't really crave sweets—unless you count the time I was expecting my first child and ended up baking seven cakes in one day while licking every spoon and bowl in sight. But that was many uncomfortable pounds ago. Let's don't dwell on that.

Now that I've returned to sanity, I thought I would just try to drink unsweetened tea, but I found it to be too bitter. I've tried adding a tiny smidgen (or "tee-ninesy," as one Southern friend says) of sugar, fake sugar (yuck), and a bevy of other flavorings, but nothing works.

> My mother always said:
> No coffee or tea
> Before you are twenty;
> But water and milk
> You need to drink plenty.

She recited that almost every day of my life as she poured me a big glass of whole milk for breakfast, lunch, and dinner, seven days a week, until I broke free for college and discovered new beverage options.

Since I don't drink tea, I rarely make it either. Tea drinkers have their own formulas down and can make it without even measuring. I have to count each tea bag and carefully measure water and sugar to the last grain, but since I don't like it, I can never really tell if I got it right or not. And since no one in the South can legally have a guest walk through their door without a big pitcher of cold sweet tea waiting in the refrigerator (usually next to the insulin), I've learned to turn to my friend Milo for help.

In the name of Southern hospitality, a belle's gotta do what a belle's gotta do.

So when I've said the obligatory, "Y'all come see us sometime," and they take me seriously and respond with, "Okay, how's about next Tuesday afternoon?", or when I invite people over for dinner, I first trot myself down to the Piggly Wiggly and pick up a gallon of the popular Milo's

Iced Tea. Then I bring it home and pour it into my crystal pitcher. There you go. I just made tea.

Let me rephrase that. I just made tea (go into that pitcher).

I'm not trying to trick anyone. It's just that it would be totally tacky to plop a big plastic jug on the table. It would be the equivalent of bringing the Colonel's fried chicken to the church's dinner on the grounds and leaving it in the bucket! What kind of savage do you think I am? Seriously. People would discuss me for decades yet to come.

Milo's headquarters are in Bessemer, Alabama, and first started as part of the Milo hamburger chain. The popularity of the tea grew until the tea side split from the burger side to concentrate on wider distribution methods.

Now, I know I can't be the only one who uses Milo's at their house, because Piggly Wiggly always stocks quite a bit of the Southern brew. Who else out there uses my tea "recipe?" I've been told so many tea drinkers love Milo's that even the most capable tea makers often let Milo do the brewing.

If I could somehow convince other non-tea drinkers to confess their Southern sin, then perhaps we could all get together sometime and sip our iced waters on the porch together in a kind of a support group. I'd provide lemon and fresh mint, but no sugar. And I'm sure we'd still be the sweetest group in town.

# Velveeta, I Know You Not

It was a harsh reality I wasn't ready to accept. My children had been raised in the "New South" and there was no one to blame but myself. My son looked at the kitchen counter with a mix of intrigue and disgust and asked, "What is it?"

"What do you mean? It's Velveeta," I told him, knowing good and well my son was joking. But the thing is, he wasn't.

Southerners are forever being placed at the top of such lists as the Most Unhealthy-Overweight-Sickly-Early-Dying People in the country (Woo! We're #1! We're #1!) so there's a new generation of us who have been attempting to raise our children without (many) fried foods or (much) lard or (too many) creamy soup casseroles. Our children have lower cholesterol, stronger bones, and healthier hearts than those who were brought up on traditional Southern fare. But as Granny used to say, "Somethin' just ain't right."

We've created little homogenized monsters who don't know the pleasures of an orange brick of processed cheese product, especially when plopped into a Crock-Pot and stirred over low heat with a can of Ro-Tel mixed in. Bacon, grits, and biscuits have been replaced by granola, fresh fruit, and whole-wheat toast. I honestly think that in twenty-one years of marriage, I've only owned one can of Crisco and it lasted for about three years. There is a Mason jar of bacon drippings in my refrigerator, but it's there mostly out of obligatory habit and doesn't get filled nor emptied often.

When I do fry foods like okra, chicken, or squash, it's a rare treat. I don't think I ever had a meal at my grandmother's house where there wasn't something fried, buttered, or smothered. There were always at least two kinds of bread on her table, either biscuits or cornbread and just plain, sliced white bread stacked on a plate. I'll make cornbread every now and then, mostly to accompany a pot of (turkey) chili in the winter, but rarely biscuits and never, ever white bread.

But not wanting to be a terrible mom and cut my boys off from all that is good, I decided to make the best football-watching snack ever invented. I have a friend who lives in Seattle who says it's difficult to find Velveeta in her stores, let alone anyone who has heard of Velveeta-Ro-Tel dip. She thinks it's a Southern snack, but I can't imagine the rest of the country hasn't caught on yet.

Since I've raised my boys in a semi-healthy house, one kid thinks a good snack is a big carrot and the other prefers strawberries, so when I decided to make the Velveeta dip, they looked at me like I was trying to poison them. "What do you do with it?" asked one. "Do you eat it like soup?" the other wanted to know. I put chips in a big bowl and told them to dig in, then stepped back to watch.

Hallelujah! The angels began to sing. They thought I was some type of culinary muse who had brought cheesiness to a new level. But then something strange happened. After a minute of stuffing their faces, they stopped. "Don't you want some more?" I asked. "No thanks, it's really heavy," said the oldest. The younger one agreed and said it was really good but wanted to know if I had some sliced bell peppers to dip into the cheese instead of chips.

The new faces of Southern connoisseurs have the best of both eras. They can occasionally enjoy the traditional richer dishes but know to balance it all with newer, slimmed-down fare. And unlike their poor great-grandparents, who only lived to be 89 and 102, my kids will live long and healthy lives.

# Everything Old Is Roux Again

A church to which I once belonged assembled a cookbook and asked all members to contribute their favorite recipes. Knowing the longevity of such books, my mother wisely warned me not to submit recipes that contained the phrase "Open a can of . . ." She said it would haunt me for the rest of my days.

Instead, a safe and classic recipe to have attached to your name for perpetuity should begin with enticing, mouthwatering words. Something like "First, you make a roux." I took her advice, submitted our family's treasured Shrimp and Sausage Gumbo recipe, and years later I'm still getting compliments.

Roux is the staple of many good Gulf Coast culinary creations. Some étoufées, sauces, gravies, and, of course, our beloved gumbo all start with a roux. So along with making a good hushpuppy, new cooks along the Gulf Coast are taught the art of the roux early on. Yet there are wonderful cooks who still fear it, anticipating great complications. But if you've grown up clinging to the apron of an experienced cook, and you own a good cast-iron skillet (and bless your heart if you don't), then you too can "do a roux."

The first lesson I ever had in the kitchen was to always close the silverware drawer before cracking an egg nearby. I wasn't allowed back in the kitchen for a long time after that, but when I was finally permitted to return for the second lesson, I learned to make a roux.

Cooks will vary the basics of oil versus butter depending on the desired color and depth of the roux. But once you get the hang of it, and the correct rhythm—heat, heat; stir, stir; whisk, whisk—magic begins. And one more requirement: you can't be colorblind. "Blonde," "copper," and "brunette" don't refer to the charming belles on the front porch.

Knowing all about roux, I was somewhat surprised to hear of an old recipe using a roux that was new to me. It's something that good Southern country women have cooked forever, and yet it had somehow escaped me.

Ever heard of tomato gravy?

At a family reunion, the wife of a second cousin once removed and my aunt were talking about pouring tomato gravy over biscuits. Why had I never heard of tomato gravy? I asked them how it was made and they looked at me like I had just asked how to whistle "Dixie." What planet was I from?

I marched straight over to my mother and asked how she could have made such an error in raising me. She said Daddy had never really liked tomato gravy, so like many other good things, the man's preferences dominated the menu, and the legacy of the sauce in my family had died.

I hurried home and started researching tomato gravy, only to find that it is basically a roux with diced tomatoes thrown in. Seriously? That seemed too simple to be any good. Sometimes the butter or oil is replaced or strengthened with finger-snappin'-good and cholesterol-enhancing bacon grease. *Mmmm.*

This is the kind of dish you don't need a recipe for, so it won't ever make the pages of a church cookbook, and forget about it ever being in the Junior League books. Tomato gravy is in the same category as Jell-O or grits. You should just instinctively know how to make it.

I gave the tomato gravy a try and ate it over hot biscuits, and I loved it. My family did too, except for one picky teenager who doesn't like to eat anything red except for M&Ms, but he's not normal.

Now I have a new topping for biscuits and a new reason to love a good roux. Which goes to show you, everything old is "roux" again!

### Old-Fashioned Tomato Gravy

Born of the Southern tradition of using what is on hand and not letting a drop of precious bacon grease or a single tomato go to waste, different versions of this recipe have been around for generations. There are hundreds of ways to make tomato gravy, using whatever items are in your pantry or garden. Should you add the onions or not? Do you like bell peppers in your gravy? Well, today yes, but maybe next week no. You can use chicken broth, water, cream, or milk as your liquid. Just about anything goes.

The basic formula for this Southern staple is to use your bacon grease, full of rich flavor, to make a roux then add in diced tomatoes for a fresh tanginess. Tomatoes from the garden are always preferred, but don't fret if canned is all you have.

Tomato gravy is traditionally served over fresh, fluffy, hot biscuits, but it is also good over meatloaf, mashed potatoes, or even green beans.

Here is the basic recipe. I add onions and bell peppers and often enhance the grease with a little bit of butter, both for richness and to increase the amount of roux.

¼ cup bacon drippings (A 16-oz. package of bacon usually produces approximately 1 cup of bacon drippings.)
¼ cup all-purpose flour
Butter as needed
½ cup diced onion (optional)
½ cup diced bell pepper (optional)
1 cup chicken broth (or substitute milk, cream, or water)
2 medium tomatoes, peeled and chopped (or substitute 1 can of diced or stewed tomatoes)
2-3 tbsp. tomato paste (optional, for a thicker gravy)
Salt and pepper to taste

Before you start your roux, go ahead and sauté the diced onion and/or pepper if you are choosing to use them.

After frying bacon in what I hope is a good cast-iron skillet, remove the bacon and blend the flour in to make a light to medium roux the color of peanut butter. If you don't have enough grease, you can add butter until the correct consistency is achieved. Just balance the amount of fat (grease and butter) with the flour. And remember, the secret to a good roux is to keep stirring!

Next, you may add the sautéed onion and diced bell pepper if desired. Stir until onion and pepper are tender. Add the broth (or your preferred liquid) and keep stirring. Finally, when the roux has been blended with the liquid, slowly add tomatoes. Reduce heat to a low simmer. Cover for 5 minutes while giving an occasional stir, until the gravy is blended and heated through. Add tomato paste to thicken up the gravy, if desired, and season with salt and pepper. Enjoy!

### Shrimp and Sausage Gumbo

4 cups diced Conecuh Sausage or other smoked sausage
1 cup diced onion
1 cup diced green bell pepper
1 cup diced red bell pepper
½ cup chopped celery
2 tbsp. minced garlic
½ cup fresh corn cut off cob, or canned
⅓ cup butter
⅓ cup all-purpose flour
4 cups chicken broth (or substitute seafood or shrimp
    stock), divided
1 bay leaf
3 cups diced tomatoes
1 lb. raw shrimp, peeled and deveined

Cook sausage in a cast-iron skillet over medium heat until brown. Reserving the drippings in the skillet, use a slotted spoon to remove the sausage. Drain sausage on a paper towel and set aside. Sauté onion, peppers, celery, garlic, and corn in the sausage drippings, stirring occasionally until soft. Remove vegetables and set aside.

Add butter to the remaining drippings in the skillet. Once the butter has melted, slowly mix in the flour, stirring constantly until you make a chocolate-colored roux. Set aside.

Pour 3 cups of the broth into a large stockpot over medium heat, then slowly spoon in the roux mixture. Whisk to completely blend until there are no lumps. Add bay leaf and reduce heat to a simmer. Once completely blended, add tomatoes. Cover and simmer for 5-10 minutes, stirring occasionally until tomatoes begin to break down.

Add the cooked sausage and vegetable mixture to the

stockpot. Cover and simmer over low heat for 10-15 minutes, stirring occasionally.

Ten minutes before serving, add the remaining cup of broth and the shrimp. Shrimp will cook quickly; don't overcook them or they will become tough. Stir the gumbo until shrimp are pink and cooked through.

Serve over hot rice. Hey, that's nice.

# Lane Cake Is a Lame Cake

In my never-ending quest to sprinkle a touch of class on our dinner table conversation, I approached the topic of current events and informed my son and husband that the Lane cake had recently been named the official State Dessert of Alabama, to which my son replied, "*Lame* cake?" and my husband said, "Is that all the legislature has to do?"

Sigh . . . here we go again.

But after I pondered my son's misinterpretation, I had to agree this cake is kind of "lame" when it comes to representing the spirit of sweetness found in Alabama. I'm sure some consider Lane cake to be a marvelous concoction, but there must be others like me who view it more as a "no, thank you" kind of treat.

Yes, the recipe, which originated in Clayton, Alabama, and was created by Emma Lane—who I'm sure was a darling, charming, and caring lady, not to mention a marvelous cook—uses native Alabama pecans, but the version I'm familiar with also includes coconut, which when shredded always makes me think I'm eating Easter basket grass, and anyway it screams "Hawaii" or "South Florida," not Alabama.

The other ingredient I take great issue with is the addition of raisins, from California no doubt. Only shifty people think it's okay to sneak raisins into any sort of dessert. How many innocent people have mistaken raisins for chocolate chips in cookies, only to gag on the rotten, shriveled-up little grape? Who as a child didn't suck the chocolate off and spit the raisin out?

My mother tried to get me to eat raisins by telling me they would give me "thick blood," as if that were a desirable quality. *Mmm.* Nothing like freaking out your little girl to trick her into eating rubbery beads of goo. And even though I can't imagine eating a raisin on purpose, I too fell into the mom trap of trying to convince my own children to eat raisins. I put the tiny little red boxes in their lunches every day, and when they came home unopened, I just left them in there for the next day. My sons now claim they had the same two boxes of raisins for eight years in a row.

Another great concern and reason to question the Lane cake as our state dessert is that it also contains enough hooch that if it were used as a birthday cake, the candles would spark a small explosion, which could prove to be risky in a state full of (public) teetotalers. When Alabama's largest religious denomination can't openly carry this cake to the dinner on the grounds, that's not representative of all Alabamians. "I'll fly away" indeed.

Just because the cake was mentioned by Harper Lee in her iconic *To Kill a Mockingbird* doesn't mean it should automatically have a place of honor in the Montgomery Hall of Fame. When Lee wrote that Miss Maudie Atkinson took a Lane cake over to welcome Aunt Alexandra, maybe it was a secret literary wink that Aunt Alexandra wasn't well liked, because isn't a true sign of genuine friendship delivering something made of delicious, rich chocolate? If not, then why don't we give our loved ones big boxes of raisins on Valentine's Day?

If you start with the basic Lane cake, then take away the gummy raisins, prickly coconut, and devil's brew, what you're left with is basically a beautiful, delicious butter pecan cake made from the state's official nut and butter from our local dairies. What could be more elegant and simple than that? Top it off with a few peaches from Clanton, and you've got yourself a true Yellowhammer delight.

More so than laws regarding health insurance or school systems, I think the issue of official state dessert should have been included on a statewide ballot, therefore allowing the citizens to make the important dessert decision. I guarantee if it was put to a public vote, there would have been a record turnout at the polls, and that would have been a truly sweet day for our Sweet Home Alabama.

# BBQ Is a Food, Not a Party in Your Backyard

I can't believe I fell for it. Friends who have transplanted themselves from "another part of the country" invited us over for "barbecue." BBQ. Bar-B-Que. However you want to spell it or say it, I was a happy camper. I think over the years barbecue has tied with fried fish as my favorite meal.

When we barbecue at our house, it's a long process with my husband doing the smoking and cooking while I mix the dry rub and make my own sauce with the secret ingredient being a couple of tablespoons of cane syrup. There was a time when the syrup came from my family's farm, but those days are gone and I have to search for other local sources. And even though I favor my concoction, I don't turn my nose up at some of the savory bottled varieties.

We are blessed to live in barbecue heaven with many good restaurants ready to do the work for us. Alabama-based Moe's, Saw's, and Dreamland are my favorites, as well as Sprayberry's in Newnan, Georgia. I'm not even opposed to Big Bob Gibson's famous white sauce when I'm in North Alabama.

I prepared for the tastiest meal of the week with my friends with great seriousness. A dark-colored shirt was a must, since barbecue is known to drip and I'm known to spill. My contribution was potato salad, a good, cool balance to the spicy sauce. The only question that remained—and I played it over in my head like a guessing game—was what type of meat would it be? Chicken? Pulled pork? Ribs? It was like trying to guess if I were getting rubies, sapphires, or emeralds. They're all fine with me!

We were greeted by our hosts and ushered to the backyard, where the grill was already puffing away, and I inhaled the smoky aroma—but something wasn't right. The air was thick with a delicious smell, but then the host lifted the grill's lid, and in slow-motion horror, I realized this was no barbecue. It was a cookout with hamburgers!

I didn't know what to say, so I just stood there in shock. My husband knew exactly what I was thinking. Since he was raised by people who are from "another part of the country," he quickly figured out why I had a tear running down my cheek and shot me a look that said, "Don't say anything; I'll explain later." I ate my burger, which was very good, and tried not to openly sulk.

Apparently, when some people say, "Let's barbecue," they really mean, "Why don't you come over for a *cookout?*" or "Come over and we will *grill* some burgers." They casually and irreverently toss the word "barbecue" around to mean all sorts of things not even remotely associated with a sauce-covered piece of slow-cooked, dry-rubbed meat.

"If I knew that you were coming, I'd have fried a cake" doesn't sound right. Just as you can't exchange the word "fried" for "baked," you can't transpose "grilling" and "barbecue." There's an art to managing the indirect heat of barbecue that differentiates it from grilling. My friend Alan is an official, certified judge in the Kansas City Barbecue Society and knows Southerners take their barbecue seriously. As he says, "I've heard discussions about barbecue with more details and seriousness than a legal document."

This disrespectful use of "barbecue" needs to stop. I'm sure if someone were picky enough, they could look it up and find that both uses are acceptable (in some places), but if you are in the South, please know when you say "barbecue," we think food, not social event in the backyard. When in Rome eat pasta, and when in the South eat barbecue. Don't "do" barbecue.

I think these anti-barbecue people know exactly what they are doing and are just poking at us. It started a few years ago with the word "frosting" being tossed out over our beloved "icing." It's hard to read a recipe these days with all the language barriers.

I'm going to invite these same friends over for polenta and give them grits and see how they like it.

# The Perfectly Picked Pecans

In many Southern cities, you can't walk a straight line without smacking into a large pecan tree. Many of our newer subdivisions and even parts of the downtown area are built on former pecan farms. While out on a walk last week, I scooped up a handful of the nuts and stuffed them deep into my coat pockets for a treat when I returned home.

But when I cracked the pecans, bits of shell flew across the kitchen counter. The meat of the nut came out in small fragments, and I was reminded of the dexterity my grandmother once used to remove the inside portion of pecans perfectly intact and unblemished. My crumbly mess would have made her smile and shake her head.

The immense pecan tree in Grandmother's backyard dropped truckloads of nuts every year. She would gather the fallen pecans, crack them open, and patiently pick out the meat with her pointy metal picker tool, then place the smooth halves in pint-size bags.

After an autumn visit, Grandmother would send me home with several bags and I would stick them in my freezer. Throughout the holiday season, I would go to these bags for my recipe needs. Pies, cookies, cornbread dressing, cakes, and sweet potato casseroles all got a generous portion of perfectly picked pecans. I would always alert my children when they ate the bounty, "These are Granny's pecans. She picked these out just for us!"

But like so many other chores completed by others, I took for granted all the time and skill it had taken for

Grandmother to come up with the end result of bulging bags of ready-to-use nuts. Until one fall, when she was no longer there to do it for me.

After Grandmother was gone, when the family gathered at her house we solemnly assembled 'round her upright freezer and quietly and slowly opened the door. As the bright light and cold air poured out in foggy clouds, we stood in awe of the neatly stacked bags of that year's frozen pecans, okra, field peas, and a half-dozen other gifts from the garden. A frozen feast was before us, sparkling with ice crystals like treasured jewels. It was the last supper, so to speak.

That year, I used the final bags of Grandmother's pecans sparingly, not wanting to run out or waste even one. The following year, I gathered my own pecans and sat for hours fumbling and mumbling not-so-nice things about how difficult it was to produce an unscarred pecan half. My bags of broken pecan fragments ended up with sharp bits of shell in them. Not what you want to find in a chewy cookie.

And did I mention Grandmother picked those pecan halves for me every year with hands twisted from arthritis?

I keep trying. I keep trying. I keep trying. I'm determined to master the perfectly picked pecan yet.

# The Joy of Cooking from a Church Cookbook

Laura Jean was asked to chair the new cookbook committee for her church in Prattville, and she's beyond thrilled. She took the words out of my mouth when she said, "I thought with the availability of recipes on the internet these days, we'd never see another church cookbook again." Everyone in the South knows the best recipes come from church cookbooks. The Junior League cookbooks come close, but with the church books, you also get a little dose of morality thrown in with the salt and pepper.

My mother once submitted a recipe to our church cookbook for Watergate Cake, and the ladies on the dessert committee called to ask if it was okay for them to change the name to Pistachio Pudding Cake because Watergate was such a "terrible time in our history." No matter that the cake was named after the hotel restaurant's featured dessert, not the unfortunate political incident.

Someone always tries to out-church the other cooks by submitting the standard recipe for a Christian home. It lists the ingredients as things like one cup of patience, two tablespoons of laughter, one cup of love, moisten with tears of sympathy, and mix with daily prayer . . . There is also the similarly irritating recipe for Scripture Cake, which makes you drag your Bible out and look up Isaiah 10:14 so you can figure out why you need two cups of it or one cup of Naham 3:12, chopped, and one tablespoon of Amos 4:5. Has anyone ever really made this? And wouldn't it get your Bible covered with sugar and flour?

For some reason, church cookbooks reflect Southerners' fascination with making food into balls. You know, sausage balls, cheese balls (both Parmesan and cheddar), and balls made from shrimp, cucumber, olives, oranges, or peanut butter. Chili porcupine balls were always a hit at the Esther Circle luncheons, held in the fellowship hall on the third Tuesday of every month.

The biggest shock to ever hit Magnolia Grove Baptist Church was when the scandalous recipe for Saucy Cocktail Balls showed up. The committee couldn't decide which was worse, "saucy," "cocktail," or "balls," and the rumor is that they finally threw their hands up in disgust and included it. After all, it was the pastor's wife who submitted the recipe in the first place. (But they drew the line at Polynesian Breasts).

The older cookbooks, printed before the 1990s, were full of healthy salad recipes, and when I say "healthy," let's just admit they were really desserts containing ingredients like cream cheese, brown sugar, and Ritz Crackers. One Cherry Salad recipe, submitted by Mrs. John Fishembacker, of the Gadsden Fishembackers, included one can of cherry pie filling, condensed milk, Cool Whip, marshmallows, and a can of pineapple.

The newer books gave a nod to foreign missions by including exotic recipes like Oriental Salad and Enchilada Casserole, which somehow managed to incorporate a can of cream of mushroom and a can of cream of chicken soup, along with Velveeta. Totally authentic Mexican food, right? The newer books also modernized the contributors' names and instead of the old-fashioned "Mrs. John Smith," they came a long way, baby, and contributors were listed as "Mrs. John Smith (Vera)."

Always thirsty but mindful of those who are "weak for the drink," there were twenty-four different punch recipes, all of them including a different flavor of Jell-O so you could color coordinate with the bridesmaids' dresses.

Of course, the best section of all church cookbooks is casseroles. Church folks instinctively know how to make a casserole and wisely stock cases of creamed soups in their pantries, ready to go in case there's a death, birth, or illness. Three versions of Company Casserole are listed in one of my books: one topped with crushed cornflakes, one with crushed saltines, and the third with Chinese noodles, once again giving a nod to the memory of dear Lottie Moon.

The joy of cooking from a church cookbook may not be the actual recipes, although there are some big winners in those pages, but the true happiness found is seeing the names of those who took the time to share their favorite recipes, which you've eaten for years at covered dish luncheons and dinner on the grounds. A former Sunday School teacher or someone who taught you in Vacation Bible School, the church organist or the librarian who let you check out five books at once, even though she knew you were going to read them during church, will have shared a favored dish. Certainly in heaven there will be a cookbook committee. They'll be non-judgmental and accepting of everyone, so there will be a smorgasbord of international recipes, and no one will blink an eye at the most popular dessert, Watergate Cake, submitted by Mrs. R. Nixon (Patricia).

# I Love Gas Station Food

Forgive me, for I have sinned against the handbook of fancy, Southern, ladylike behavior. I can't help myself, but I love sneaking off and eating gas station food.

I'm not referring to the new trend in gas stations where they've installed real restaurants with professional chefs. Such places have sprung up in Texas and reportedly have lines out the door waiting on gourmet meals that rival five-star restaurants. What I crave—only every now and then, I promise—is the salty, crispy, greasy decadence only found under the heat lamp at Paw-Paw's Gas-n-Go.

I'm honestly not nearly as persnickety as my friends think, but why bother them with my secret of driving down to Magnolia Springs to a secluded station where on Fridays I can get a tank of gas, enjoy a plate of fried catfish, and wash it down with a cold Yoo-hoo? In between jaunts to scoop up Styrofoam cups full of addictive "redneck crack" (boiled peanuts), I offer penance for my sins by eating healthy. I really and truly drink smoothies made of beets, pineapple, and spinach, so indulging every now and then on a taquito that's been basking beneath the glow of an orange light isn't so bad, is it?

Human nature makes us all thrill seekers on one level or the other and since I'll never fling myself out of an airplane, risking my life on a sausage that's been spinning on metal rollers gives me just the sense of boldness I need. There's also the added peril of running into a fellow member of the Committee for the Preservation of Loveliness, which would be utterly horrifying. If any of them caught me hiding behind the hot nacho display, dabbing chemically manufactured cheese sauce from the corner of my mouth, I'd never live it down. They would be forced to discuss me and take action at the next meeting.

Since everyone has to have standards of some sort, even I've learned to draw the line at the big jar of pickled eggs next to the cash register. First of all, the only time I tried one, it turned my mouth inside out and sucked the breath out of me. Next, I'm suspicious of just how long they've been floating around in that brine. The day I heard Andy Griffith died, I had just pulled into the station, and when I relayed the news to the girl who was filling the jar, she went into some sort of shock and plopped the eggs down in there all at once, causing a few to get dinged-up. To this very day, I can recognize them as the same eggs from all those years ago because I noticed one had a mark on it that looked like Barney Fife. Spooky coincidence, if you ask me.

The other problem with eating gas station food is the high turnover rate of the employees, who can be very temperamental. Just when you think you've found a good gas station, the cook will up and leave and the entire groove will be thrown off. A few months ago, I stopped at a place on my "favorites" list, somewhere near Prattville, and thought I was getting my beloved chicken fingers, but when I took the first bite, I knew something was amiss. Come to find out, the longtime cook had quit that Tuesday because the owner decided to spiff things up and add little cups of edamame to the menu. The cook said there was no way she was working under such new-aged conditions. By Saturday, she had found a better job cooking down at the Flora-Bama, where she was also crowned Miss February Beach Babe. It worked out well for her, but I was left with dry, bland chicken that I tossed out the window to be discovered later by some unfortunate raccoons.

What I'm trying to tell you is if you run into me down at the Fuel-a-Rama and I don't speak, just know it's because I'm ashamed and probably hiding a bag of fried macaroni and cheese bites. Peace be with me and Lord have mercy on my stomach.

# What Kind of Mother Doesn't Fry Okra?

Every now and then, we all deserve a little reward or treat. When my son was thirteen years old, he successfully passed a very difficult test, and I told him, "Let's celebrate! What would you like for a treat?" I thought for certain he would ask to be taken to the ice cream shop, but, instead, he piped up, "I want fried okra!" Definitely not what I had in mind.

I tried to redirect his focus by reasoning, "You know a waffle cone is so good when it's filled with chocolate chip ice cream," but he wanted none of it. "No, ma'am, I want fried okra." I was pulling for the ice cream, not because I wanted some (which I did), but because it only takes five minutes to run into the ice cream shop and grab a cone, and it takes forever to fry up a mess of okra.

Cutting, dipping, breading, frying, draining. Then the entire stove and countertop are covered with little grease marks. Even if you haven't ruined your shirt on the areas the apron doesn't cover, you'll probably have experienced the worst pain Southern cooks know, which is the sting of hot, popping grease landing on your arms or hands.

Thank goodness, I finally had a deep cast-iron pot suitable for frying. For years, I'd only had two large cast-iron skillets, one from each grandmother, but both were too shallow to adequately fry anything. We have the Southern-required outdoor frying gear for fish, hushpuppies, turkey, or whatever else we can think to throw in there, but everyone knows smaller food items like okra, zucchini, and chicken legs are indoor projects.

Some families hover over Grandma's jewelry box after the funeral. My family starts eyeing the cast-iron collection. We know that, like wine and live oak trees, cast iron is better as it ages. Thank goodness I've had the two skillets, since I use them almost every single day. The newer, deep pot came from an aunt who took pity on me since I didn't have anything appropriate to hold hot, scalding oil. I really don't fry food that often, not only because of the mess, but also because along with the gift of the skillets, one grandmother also passed along her naturally high cholesterol levels. Mostly, my skillets are used for healthy stir-fry vegetables or pineapple upside-down cakes.

My husband's family never used cast-iron cookware (bless his mama's New York heart), and the first month we were married, I caught him feverishly scrubbing one of my skillets with *steel wool!* He quickly learned the art of proper cast-iron care and also gained a new appreciation for the art of a proper hissy fit.

Since I had the required equipment, I had no good excuse. I felt guilty. How many kids request vegetables for their reward for a job well done? So honey, if my sweet boy wants okra, then I'm going to fry him okra. When he grows up, I don't want him telling his wife I never cooked okra for him. What kind of mother won't fry okra?

Someday, he'll tell his wife about how good my fried okra is. She'll be so impressed, and I know she'll also be the kind of good girl who appreciates my perfectly seasoned cast iron. But what will happen if she comes from a family who doesn't know how to use cast iron? Well, God help us, because then we'll have bigger fish to fry.

## Fried Okra

1 lb. fresh okra
2 eggs
1 cup buttermilk (optional)
Dash hot sauce (optional)
1 cup cornmeal
½ cup all-purpose flour
Salt and pepper to taste

Wash okra and cut into bite-size, round pieces, discarding tips. In a bowl, mix together eggs. To make a thinner "bath," you may add buttermilk and hot sauce to the eggs. Add okra pieces to the egg bath and stir to coat.

In a shallow dish, mix together cornmeal, all-purpose flour, and salt and pepper to taste. Plop the okra pieces into the cornmeal mixture in small batches and toss to coat.

Heat vegetable oil in a deep pan to 375 degrees. My mom showed me the trick of placing a kernel of popcorn in the oil. When it pops, it's ready! Fry the okra, turning until lightly brown and cooked through. Drain on paper towels and serve while hot.

Consider yourself rewarded for a job well done!

# V.
# Our Divine Southern Churches

Churches, cathedrals, chapels, and synagogues are big parts of our lives in the South. It matters not what your denomination is, we take comfort in knowing our friends and neighbors see the larger picture and share a conviction to love, help, and honor one another. We worship with our friends and grow to love them like family. It's rumored that when Southerners get to heaven, if there's a long line at the pearly gates, we get a fast pass. But watch out for the Mississippi folks. They think they get to cut in front of the entire line every day.

(Courtesy Robert M. Tarabella)

237

# Why I Teach Vacation Bible School

The word "vacation" in Vacation Bible School is a trick that makes sweet church ladies volunteer for the king-daddy of all summer spectacles. No longer a quiet week of coloring pictures of Moses while nibbling crunchy and creamy Oreo cookies, Vacation Bible School, or VBS, is now a production that makes *Star Wars* seem like a backyard puppet show. Just under five hundred children and volunteers showed up at our church this year for a razzle-dazzle good time.

Costumes and decorations, soundtracks, and special lighting add to the experience of being in the desert for forty days and nights, and when the fog machine is added the next day, we're transported to a rocking boat on the Sea of Galilee.

More coordinated than the U.S. Army, the VBS Mom Squad mans their stations for skits, songs, science experiments, and even themed snacks. Yogurt with a message? Yep. The snack lady told us, "The granola on top is rocky and hard like our lives can sometimes get. But the yogurt underneath is sweet and smooth, which is how our lives can be with Jesus."

Would it kill them to find a good lesson inside an Oreo?

After I was too old to attend VBS, I followed the natural progression of church ladies and became a volunteer. At first, I was only a teenage helper, but then I achieved the much-anticipated and honorable position of group leader. Since then, I've also led the music, recreation, and games, dressed as Bible characters, told stories, led field trips, and served snacks.

Even though I'm a veteran when it comes to Bible School, I'm still completely surprised each year at how worn out I am at the end of each day. The children are adorable, but they will suck every ounce of energy from your saved soul. When I taught in public schools, I could immediately get the undivided attention of the wildest of classrooms by slamming a book on the desk and giving them the evil eye, but at VBS, I'm forced to use my church manners and be peaceful, kind, gentle, good, patient, and all that other stuff that is expected in God's house. It's utterly exhausting for me to be so sweet around that many children.

Every summer, God shows me His sense of humor when He sends little boys into my group who would make the preacher cuss. You know the ones. They'll find a paper clip on the floor and bend it to form a weapon for little girls' legs. They make naughty things out of the popsicle sticks and spin around on the floor during the prayer. Bathroom sinks get backed up with paper towels, and, no lie, one year I had a little boy who wrote his name on the bathroom wall—and it wasn't with a crayon. Obviously, my righteousness wasn't the only thing that sprung a leak that day.

By the end of the week, the children have finally learned the daily routine, the volunteers have reconciled themselves to feeding their own children drive-through hamburgers five days in a row, and the closing assembly is minutes away. We're all sitting crossed-legged on the hard floor beneath a tent in faux Jerusalem when the roughest of the boys comes and sits next to me and quietly says, "I'm kind of like Jonah."

"You mean you're stuck inside a big fish?"

"No, I mean that sometimes I don't do what God tells me to do. But when I finally listen, everything turns out to be really good."

I take a deep breath, dab the corners of my eyes, and haul my weary self up off the floor and go sign up to teach Vacation Bible School again the next year.

With or without the Oreo cookies.

# Go to Church or the Devil Will Get You

*Yes, there really is a sign on Interstate 65 in Alabama that says, "Go to Church or the Devil Will Get You!" It's on private property and was erected so long ago that an entire generation has grown up seeing it on the way to the beach or on a trip to Granddaddy's house. Since most Southerners respect the rights of the individual to do what they please with their land, most people don't get upset, and many actually love it.*

*When I wrote this story, I got plenty of feedback from people sharing their memories of how they felt when they saw the sign, and I was pleasantly surprised that the comments were mostly positive. I wasn't really sure how my story would be received since it's one of the more directly religious pieces I've done, but I think my readers appreciate honesty, and most were able to identify with it in one way or the other. I heard from many who said they read it aloud to their Sunday School classes or prayer groups, and one man even said seeing that sign for years finally brought him to the door of a church and resulted in the healing of his broken family.*

*So, I guess the intent of the sign was a success. It sure got us all talking.*

Living in a state that literally has a sign on Interstate 65 that says, "Go to Church or the Devil Will Get You!" has often made me wonder exactly what my motives were for hauling my children to a place I knew was full of hypocritical, sinning, yet loving, forgiven, and hopeful people. Why have I knocked myself out all these years taking my children to church?

My husband and I always laughed at the song "Easy Like Sunday Morning" because locating the missing shoe, slicking down cowlicks, and checking pockets for small reptiles and/or fireworks was anything but easy when we were trying to make it to Sunday School by 9:45 with two little boys in tow. It wasn't uncommon for us to arrive in the parking lot with someone in the car pouting and a few others thinking purely evil thoughts about everyone else in the car, and by the time we took a deep breath, smoothed our clothes, and walked through the door, we all needed Jesus to whop us upside the head.

In all honesty, one early benefit of taking our boys to church was being able to hand them over to the sweet ladies in the nursery while we got to sit with other calm, non-food-throwing adults for an hour. Literal heavenly peace for young parents.

Sure, tradition also played a role in our commitment because although our ancestors represented many different denominations, they all passed down their strong faith. Without doubt, there were a few pirates, cattle rustlers, and bootleggers amongst the bunch, but overall their salvation was steadfast. My husband and I decided we weren't going to be the weak link in the long, strong chain of faith. If our culture turns its back on God, we don't want the blame. Knowing we did our part in continuing the legacy was crucial.

Ours is a typical modern family geographically separated from real kinfolk, and church members helped our children develop goodness, patience, peace, and kindness. Genetics may not have connected us, but we're family nonetheless. Words of wisdom often take root and grow stronger when delivered by someone other than the parents, so I was grateful when the children's and youth leaders with far more experience than I stepped in to guide my boys in positive ways when my own efforts flopped.

The activities of a church youth group put the command "Feed my sheep" into action, which has been a joy to watch. My boys had the opportunity to participate in meaningful projects and learned firsthand what Jesus meant when he said to feed the hungry, care for the sick, and visit those in prison.

They've also learned to tune out the rhetoric of hate and instead offer love and kindness to those who are different, then further developed this compassion by lending a hand to those who live in poverty, when other teens only saw it on TV.

The feeling of being connected to something greater— not only to the local church, but to all believers—reinforces a child's feeling of belonging and having a purpose. On Sunday mornings, it's amazing to know there are others around the world in majestic cathedrals, dusty country chapels, and forbidden home gatherings saying and believing the exact same words we say. When the world is going crazy with wars and senseless violence, knowing something greater is in control comforts and inspires us to be and do better.

But it's more than social justice and earthly kindness. Taking my children to church has built their relationship with God and other believers who are part of the big fire that reignites our embers when we start to fade.

I'm just now beginning to see the first fruit from all the laborious years of hauling my sons to the church for one activity or the other. With a few bumps along the way, they're on the right path to becoming awesome, Godly men. So I guess that's why I took them to church all these years. That, and not wanting the devil to get them on Interstate 65.

# The Nursery's Not My Gift

I just wanted to hold a baby. I wanted to snuggle my face into its chubby neck and smell baby powder and lotion. My two boys are giant teenagers and in no way resemble anything I could hold or rock to sleep on the front porch, and, actually, these days I'd fit in their arms better than they in mine. Since none of our friends have babies and the children next door are old enough to talk your head clean off and won't sit still longer than a New York minute, I came up with a great plan.

Armed with the secret weapon of eye-batting, I managed to talk my husband into volunteering with me in the church nursery. One hour each Sunday, we'd be able to play with all the roly-poly babies then hand them back to their grateful parents. We'd been there, done that, and were more than glad to help the next wave of sleep-deprived young couples.

We didn't know that these days you can't just show up at the nursery and tell them that because you haven't lost or killed your own children, you're qualified to help. Now, before you step foot into God's Little Garden, there are fourteen forms to complete, requiring a list of relatives, recent diseases, political and theological leanings, as well as fingerprints and background checks that extend to a reference from your first-grade substitute music teacher. After we were approved (in spite of my husband's cousin Vinny), we were ready for snuggle action.

Assigned to the older baby and toddler room, I instantly bonded with the cutest girl, dressed in a fluffy green dress.

She had white ruffled socks and tiny black patent shoes, which were appropriate because it was a few weeks yet until Easter. A green bow was snuggled in her curls and she beamed at me with huge blue eyes.

"Oh, you precious darlin'!" I scooped her up and headed toward the rocking chair, but this babe had other plans. She didn't want to be rocked, walked, or patted. She didn't want to play, swing, or sing. She wanted to kick her seasonally appropriate shoes into my gut and scream—not a "missing my mommy" whimper but more of a "practicing to be a hormonal, squealing teenage girl" kind of holler that would have scared the beard off Jesus.

My husband found a dream of a round-faced little boy, who stretched out his chubby arms to be held then proceeded to barf about four gallons onto my husband's shirt and tie. This made the other babies cry, which was a convenient ruckus since my husband may or may not have said a non-church-approved word at that moment.

To distract them, we passed out animal crackers, which somehow transformed into gobs of pasty goo that the tykes smeared not only on themselves, but in each other's hair and onto the rug and all the toys.

"Our boys never acted like this."

"Something must be wrong with these kids."

"What if they're all coming down with something?"

"I can't take off from work next week, you know."

The hour-long nursery incarceration ended with every baby in the room needing a fresh diaper. So as not to be tacky, I'll just say if it's not your own baby, it's EPA-classified toxic waste.

"How did we ever do this?"

"What kind of diet are these kids on?"

"I think I'm going to cry or throw up myself."

"Promise me you're too old to ever have another baby again."

"Don't talk about how old I am."

"What? I can't hear you over all the screaming."

We never made it back to the nursery because we discovered it wasn't our "gift." We also went home and had a discussion with our boys on yet another serious danger of giving us grandchildren too early.

And for the first time in a long time, I was satisfied with the sweetness of my teenagers' necks.

# Carrying the Bible

Churches throughout the South have wrapped up another year of Vacation Bible School, which always makes me think of my own happy days spent at VBS. Well, they were mostly happy.

Every morning, before we would enter the church for the opening assembly, Mr. Jones, our church's Director of Education, would step outside and ceremoniously choose three children who would be the flag and Bible bearers during the morning ceremonies. It was all very formal back then. Nowadays, it's a screaming, dancing free-for-all, but we were still in the time when formality reigned.

After we were seated in the pews, the three favored children would carry the American flag, Christian flag, and Bible down the aisle in a formal procession to the front of the church, and at the specified moment, they would step forward as we all stood and pledged in unison. It was a very big deal.

Then, the four magic piano chords (if you heard them, you surely remember them and may hum them to yourself now) would play, and we knew that was our signal to be seated. The flag and Bible bearers were then allowed to sit on the front pew by themselves.

More than anything in the world, I wanted to carry that Bible. Other than being Miss America, it was my main goal in life.

The heavy flags would have tipped me over, but that Bible was perfect and the ultimate in responsibility. The pledge to the Bible was saved for last and the bearer of God's word got to stand smack in the center of the church, just beneath the cross, and lift the Bible high over their head for all to see. Honoring God and performance art all rolled into one gig—if ever there was a task made for me, this was it.

Mr. Jones always saw me wildly waving my hand to volunteer along with the other children, and after a few years of looking right through me, he finally leaned over and whispered, "Let's let some of these other little children have a chance." A cold chill ran down my spine because I knew that was code for "You can't be chosen to do anything because your daddy is the Minister of Music."

Smacked down again because of my checkered family relations! I was always being told I couldn't do things because the other children had to come first. They were often referred to as the "poor little children." But what about me? As the minister's child, I felt like the ultimate poor little child.

For crying out loud, I had sat through every boring minute of adult choir practice and knew all the words to Handel's "Messiah" by the time I was three years old. I had to show up early and stay late for every revival meeting and had to play the piano for the Sunday School classes while all my friends were giggling on the back row. If you asked me, I was a shoo-in for "poor little child" who deserved some Bible-bearing action.

After a few more years of watching others carry the Bible, it was finally my last day of eligibility. I had just finished the fifth grade and it was the final day of VBS, the last shot at holding that Bible I would ever have. Mr. Jones stepped out into the bright sun and began to scan the crowd. I just knew he would understand my predicament. I had practiced marching around my bedroom with the Bible held high over my head, but would all my hard work be in vain?

The children went wild, and Mr. Jones' blue eyes landed on my very earnest face with giant teeth. I tried to exude the right mix of sweetness, responsibility, and holiness. He smiled, then moved on to Tammy Sue, who stood to my left. In a very sweet voice, Mr. Jones said, "Tammy Sue, would you like to be the Bible bearer today?"

Seriously? Tammy Sue? She didn't even want to be at Bible School. She wore short-shorts and feathered her hair. If I had been a Catholic, I would have had to go straight to confession because I seriously considered tripping Tammy Sue as she walked down that aisle. I figured the Holy Bible would fly up into the air and I could make a diving catch to save it, run heroically to the front of the church, and start the pledge before Mr. Jones or Tammy Sue could lay a hand on me.

But, instead, I tried to apply some of the lessons I had learned that week and squished the idea deep down in my slightly, but not completely, guilty heart. I also had a flashback to a not-so-distant time when a cranky Sunday School teacher had dragged me off to my daddy's office for some totally unfounded reason, so I decided to play it cool.

So there you have it. I had perfect attendance at VBS every single year from kindergarten through fifth grade, which totals thirty days of my life, and not once was I chosen to be the Bible bearer. All I ended up with were some certificates and a pencil holder made from Popsicle sticks that said, "The last shall be first and the first shall be last." I left it on Mr. Jones' desk when he wasn't looking.

# Just a Little Bit of Trouble in a Baptist Church

The day I made my way from the front of the church to the back, by way of crawling on the floor beneath the pews, was the day that ended with a spark of revival and righteous reprimand.

Before you get excited and think this incident occurred this past year, get your head on straight. I was not quite three years old and just the right size to wiggle my way past a startled Sister Donna Jean and under the legs of snoring Mr. Joe-Don, who nearly jumped out of his skin and recovered by mumbling a half-hearted "Amen!"

It was a Sunday night service at the First Baptist Church in Florala, Alabama, where Daddy served as the Minister of Music. Mama thought it would be a good idea to spring me from the nursery and let me attend the big service so I could hear the older children's production of "The Little Lost Lamb."

After the boy playing the shepherd hollered and waved his staff around, I was scared and decided to get out of there before he started whacking people. If I'd run up the aisle, my mother would have surely caught me and put me back in the line of fire, so my escape route had to be cleverly concealed.

I meant no harm and was only trying to protect myself, so, taking a tip from watching *Hogan's Heroes* with Daddy, the under-pew route looked like a safe tunnel passageway. Slipping away from Mama was the easy part. She was busy grinning at the lambs, which I had already figured out were just kids with cotton balls glued all over them.

Pew number one was no challenge at all, and pew number two was a breeze, but beneath the third pew, I accidentally knocked over Mrs. Crowder's pocketbook and all her loose change rolled across the center aisle, along with a pack of Virginia Slims, which made her pretty mad at me for revealing her secret vice. As a result of my "outing" her, the ladies in her WMU circle offered special prayers for those who were in the clutches of nicotine entrapment at their meeting later that month.

Everything was going fine and I was developing what would become a lifelong appreciation for pretty shoes when around the seventh pew, I encountered six-year-old Carter Percy, who had been kicked out of the children's choir on account of his mean streak. Carter saw me coming and purposely swung his foot to give me a good whack on the top of my head, which made me yell, "Stop it, Carter Percy!" but it also inspired me to pick up a little speed.

Mama was torn as to what to do. Never one to ever make a scene, she crouched down low and, with a look on her face that would have made the Devil shiver, followed along the side aisle whispering, "Come here to me right now!" Did she think I was crazy? At that point I was not only having an adventure, but I was also smart enough to know this was quickly turning into a crime scene and she was the chief detective.

My journey ended as two ushers scooped me up after luring me into the vestibule with a stick of Juicy Fruit, and even though the congregation was filled with extra spirit and the offering was three times more than usual, Mama thanked me by whisking me outside and giving me a little spanking.

The clearest memory about that night was gazing up at the illuminated stained-glass windows while I was outside getting the "I'm talking to you, young lady" speech and thinking that church could be a fun place after all. Little did I know that adventure was the first, but unfortunately not the last, time I caused just a little, tiny bit of trouble in a Baptist church.

# The Joy Choir

In addition to some first-class holy rollers, Southern churches have also produced some mighty fine musicians, with many of the big-time stars giving credit to their religious roots for introducing them to the basics of music. But it doesn't matter how many Grammys these stars have won, nor how many thousands of screaming fans their concerts have attracted, because the most love they've ever felt from any crowd was the day they sang in "big church" as a member of the Joy Choir.

The Joy Choir takes the youngest and cutest little saints and teaches them the basics of making a joyful noise unto the Lord. You can find them rehearsing in churches all over Dixie on Wednesday nights, marching around the choir room, clacking rhythm sticks, and jingling bells. Their enthusiasm can be heard clear upstairs where the Lady's Prattle and Prayer group meets.

When the Joy Choir sings in church, you have to arrive early to find a good seat. Wide-eyed tykes are led to the front of the sanctuary as the congregation stretches their necks to get a good look at the cutest little Christians this side of heaven. In the old days the children wore white robes with big red bows under their chins, but nowadays it's more common to see the cuties wearing their own clothes: boys in freshly pressed shirts, some with a sharp-looking blazer and bow tie, and little girls in frilly dresses with coordinating hair bows. (Everyone knows the size of the bow reflects the love of the mama.)

There's always one child who has been blessed with the special talent of singing the loudest (and usually off-key) and is destined to someday become the county's football coach of the year. Another young'un will praise the Lord by singing and picking his nose at the same time, which horrifies his family as they vigorously shake their heads and mouth the words, "NO! STOP!" This child will someday grow up to be the Pastor. Another little girl shows her special talent by pulling her dress up over her head while singing. She will grow up to have "special talents" as well. Bless her heart.

My own son would stand on the top step of the risers and stare straight ahead, not opening his mouth during the entire song, thereby confirming his talent for monumental stubbornness. We tried every sort of parental threat and trick known to man and finally decided that if he participated like a big boy and used his big words to properly praise, then we would stop by the Gas-n-Go on the way home and buy him a Kit Kat. We didn't consider it a bribe as much as a holy business deal.

Out of all the years of listening to the Joy Choir, I'd have to say the best display of special talent came when a brother and sister were chosen to sing a duet. At the given moment, the siblings stepped forward from the choir and cautiously approached the microphone. Their angelic rendition of "Serve Him with Gladness" was going well as their parents, grandparents, and the entire church looked on. The other members of the Joy Choir stood behind them, dutifully singing the backup "Oooo" part.

No one knows for certain who started it, but with the slyness only a brother and sister could share, one "accidentally" bumped the other. It was probably completely innocent, but from that point on, instinct took over and the other gave a little push back, slightly harder. First this one, then that one, as the song continued. The two tykes kept singing while slugging, slapping, and swatting one another, never missing a note. When they finally hit the floor in a full-out, rolling tussle, the adult choir behind them and the congregation in front rose to their feet in order to see the outcome of the brawl.

Both children grew up to be highly intelligent teens and will no doubt end up having some sort of political career. The day they are sworn in, I want to be there to remind them that their special talent for "negotiations" all began in the Joy Choir.

# Author's Note

Thank you so much to all of my kind readers who inspire me with your feedback and encouragement every day. You can read more of my stories at AL.com or on my blog at leslieannetarabella.com. Be on the lookout for new collections in the future.

Many blessings to you all, especially the sparkly majorettes in this world!

*Leslie Anne*

(Courtesy Robert M. Tarabella)